Intellectual
Property Law
2012–2013

Routledge
Taylor & Francis Group

LONDON AND NEW YORK

Eighth edition published 2012
by Routledge
2 Park Square, Milton Park, Abingdon, Oxon OX14 4RN

Simultaneously published in the USA and Canada
by Routledge
711 Third Avenue, New York, NY 10017

Routledge is an imprint of the Taylor & Francis Group, an informa business

© 2012 Routledge

All rights reserved. No part of this book may be reprinted or reproduced or utilised in any form or by any electronic, mechanical, or other means, now known or hereafter invented, including photocopying and recording, or in any information storage or retrieval system, without permission in writing from the publishers.

Trademark notice: Product or corporate names may be trademarks or registered trademarks, and are used only for identification and explanation without intent to infringe.

First edition published by Cavendish Publishing Limited 1997
Seventh edition published by Routledge 2010

British Library Cataloguing in Publication Data
A catalogue record for this book is available from the British Library

ISBN: 978-0-415-68341-8 (pbk)
ISBN: 978-0-203-30065-7 (ebk)

Typeset in Rotis
by RefineCatch Ltd, Bungay, Suffolk

Printed and bound in Great Britain by
TJ International Ltd, Padstow, Cornwall

Contents

Table of Cases

Table of Statutes

Table of Statutory Instruments

Table of European Legislation

Directives

How to use this book

Welcome to this new edition of Routledge Intellectual Property Lawcards. In response to student feedback, we've added some new features to these new editions to give you all the support and preparation you need in order to face your law exams with confidence.

Inside this book you will find:

▨ NEW tables of cases and statutes for ease of reference

■ Revision Checklists

We've summarised the key topics you will need to know for your law exams and broken them down into a handy revision checklist. Check them out at the beginning of each chapter, then after you have the chapter down, revisit the checklist and tick each topic off as you gain knowledge and confidence.

1

Sources of law

Primary legislation: Acts of Parliament	■
Secondary legislation	■
Case law	■
System of precedent	■
Common law	■
Equity	■
EU law	■
Human Rights Act 1998	■

■ Key Cases

We've identified the key cases that are most likely to come up in exams. To help you to ensure that you can cite cases with ease, we've included a brief account of the case and judgment for a quick aide-memoire.

HENDY LENNOX v GRAHAME PUTTICK [1984]

Basic facts
Diesel engines were supplied, subject to a *Romalpa* clause, then fitted to generators. Each engine had a serial number. When the buyer became insolvent the seller sought to recover one engine. The Receiver argued that the process of fitting the engine to the generator passed property to the buyer. The court disagreed and allowed the seller to recover the still identifiable engine despite the fact that some hours of work would be required to disconnect it.

Relevance
If the property remains identifiable and is not irredeemably changed by the manufacturing process a *Romalpa* clause may be viable.

■ Companion Website

At the end of each chapter you will be prompted to visit the Routledge Lawcards companion website where you can test your understanding online with specially prepared multiple-choice questions, as well as revise the key terms with our online glossary.

You should now be confident that you would be able to tick all of the boxes on the checklist at the beginning of this chapter. To check your knowledge of Sources of law why not visit the companion website and take the Multiple Choice Question test. Check your understanding of the terms and vocabulary used in this chapter with the flashcard glossary.

■ Exam Practice

Once you've acquired the basic knowledge, you'll want to put it to the test. The Routledge Questions and Answers provides examples of the kinds of questions that you will face in your exams, together with suggested answer plans and a fully-worked model answer. We've included one example free at the end of this book to help you put your technique and understanding into practice.

QUESTION 1

What are the main sources of law today?

Answer plan

This is, apparently, a very straightforward question, but the temptation is to ignore the European Community (EU) as a source of law and to over-emphasise custom as a source. The following structure does not make these mistakes:

■ in the contemporary situation, it would not be improper to start with the EU as a source of UK law;

■ then attention should be moved on to domestic sources of law: statute and common law;

■ the increased use of delegated legislation should be emphasised;

■ custom should be referred to, but its extremely limited operation must be emphasised.

ANSWER

European law

Since the UK joined the European Economic Community (EEC), now the EU, it has progressively but effectively passed the power to create laws which are operative in this country to the wider European institutions. The UK is now subject to Community law, not just as a direct consequence of the various treaties of accession passed by the UK Parliament, but increasingly, it is subject to the secondary legislation generated by the various institutions of the EU.

Introduction

Intellectual property law deals with the formulation, usage and subsequent commercial exploitation of original creative labour. The areas outlined within this book form some type of proprietary protection over intangibles such as inventions and information.

Much of the debate revolves around how the boundary lines of intangible property are defined; this is an important aspect as intellectual property protects a wide and often valuable range of goods. Intellectual property is a rapidly moving and often topical area, with some of the recent debates revolving around GM food, gene patenting, peer-to-peer networks such as KaZaA and the 2005 legislation concerning the copyright regime.

It is important to 'hang' new legal developments onto the tenets of law. To this end this book contains up to date examples of recent case and statute law.

Confidential information

2

THE ACTION FOR BREACH OF CONFIDENCE – BASIC ELEMENTS

The basis for an action for breach of confidence may lie in equity or contract or at common law.

No right to privacy under English common law exists, although Art 8 of the European Convention on Human Rights seeks to guarantee a limited right with respect to the private life of individuals and families and to protect private correspondence. However, balanced against this is Art 10 which guarantees freedom of expression (see *Douglas v Hello! Ltd* [2001], (No. 3) [2003], (No. 8) [2004]).

The action for breach of confidence is broad ranging. It covers personal and technical trade secrets, knowhow and ideas.

Commentators have long discussed whether breach of confidence arises from one of the following doctrines:

- tort;
- property;
- equity;
- contract law.

This question may be of importance when a conflict of laws arises and when limitation periods are in dispute.

In *Kitechnology BV v Unicor GmbH Plastmaschinen* [1995] it was said that claims for breach of confidentiality did not arise in tort or contract, but were part of equity.

Breach of confidence is comprised almost entirely of case law; however, there is statutory recognition in s 171(1) of the Copyright, Designs and Patents Act (CDPA) 1988 and s 1 of the Official Secrets Act 1989.

CATEGORIES OF PROTECTABLE INFORMATION

To be protected, information must have 'the necessary quality of confidence about it, namely, it must not be something which is public property and public knowledge' (*per* Lord Greene MR in *Saltman Engineering Co Ltd v Campbell Engineering Co Ltd* [1963]).

Examples

Personal secrets ⟶ *Argyll v Argyll* [1967]

Commercial records ⟶ *Anton Piller KG v Manufacturing Processes Ltd* [1976]

Trade secrets ⟶ *Seager v Copydex* [1967]

Government secrets ⟶ *AG v Guardian Newspapers* [1990]

In *Coco Engineers v Clark* [1969], Megarry VC expressed the view that the doctrine of confidential information would only be used in cases of sufficient gravity, and not mere 'tittle-tattle'. Matters that are revealed to the public, such as by a court case, cease to be private (*Chantry Martin v Martin* [1953]).

A person receiving confidential information is still under an obligation of confidence, even if he already knows the information (*Johnson v Heat and Air Systems Ltd* [1941]).

However, confidentiality may still be maintained even though the information has been published, to prevent further damage through repetition (see *Schering Chemicals v Falman Ltd* [1982]).

Liability may sometimes attach to recipients who innocently acquire confidential information; liability arises at the time a party is informed of the breach of confidence (see *Stephenson, Jordan and Harrison Ltd v Macdonald and Evans* [1952]; *Printers and Finishers Ltd v Holloway (No 2)* [1965]).

▶ COCO ENGINEERS v CLARK [1969]

Facts

This case concerned the claimant who had created a moped engine, and had entered into negotiations with the defendant, with the intention that he would manufacture the engine for him. These negotiations broke down, and the defendant created his own engine which was similar to the one that the claimant had created. The claimant therefore sued for breach of confidence.

> This case is significant because of the important criteria produced by the judgment regarding breach of confidence; (a) important information capable of protection, (b) obligation of confidence and (c) risk of damage.

COCO V CLARK: THE THREE ESSENTIAL ELEMENTS THAT ESTABLISH BREACH OF CONFIDENCE

The broadly worded formulations for the elements of breach of confidence, adopted by the courts in the past, have tended to encourage claimants. In *Coco*, Megarry VC held the following to be necessary for an action:

(a) **Important information capable of protection**: the information must have a necessary element of confidentiality.

(b) **Obligation of confidence**: the information was communicated in circumstances where the confidant ought reasonably to have known that the disclosure had been made in confidence.

(c) **Risk of damage**: there is a risk of the information being used or disclosed in an unauthorised way, possibly causing damage.

The *Coco* case is an important case and is frequently cited. *Coco* partly followed the approach of the Court of Appeal in *Saltman Engineering Co Ltd v Campbell Engineering Co Ltd* [1948]. There is no need for an obligation of confidence to be in writing, as the courts have been prepared to imply terms.

Note that in the case of prototypes, ideas, personal secrets and employment, the three essential elements of *Coco* must be established **in each situation**.

Prototypes

Designs, prototypes or product samples shown to others prior to any business deal may be protected, but subject to the decision in *Carflow Products (UK) Ltd v Linwood Securities (Birmingham) Ltd and Others* [1996], where the court refused to impose an obligation of confidence on the party viewing the sample.

It was held that there are two possible approaches to the question of whether a disclosure was in confidence:

(a) subjective, that is, what did the parties themselves think they were doing by way of imposing or accepting obligations?; and

(b) objective, that is, what would a reasonable man think they were doing?

As equity looked at the conscience of the individual, the subjective view was the appropriate one.

The mere fact that a prototype was being offered for sale did not import an obligation of confidence.

In a passage from the *Coco* case, Megarry J suggested that an objective test could apply in situations where:

> ... information of commercial or industrial value is given on a businesslike basis and with some avowed common object in mind, such as a joint venture or the manufacture of articles by one party for the other.

He stated that he would regard the recipient of the information 'as carrying a heavy burden if he seeks to repel a contention that he was bound by an obligation of confidence'.

It is presumed that the reasonable man will know about other intellectual property rights when viewing a prototype, but he need not assume he is placing himself under an obligation of confidence in respect of the matter that could be protected independently.

Ideas

Ideas may be protected by confidential information (*Gilbert v Star Newspaper Co Ltd* [1894]).

A claim in confidential information may assist in situations where copyright is of no assistance (*Frazer v Thames Television* [1984] – idea for the 'Rock Follies' series).

However, in *De Maudsley v Palumbo and Others* [1996], the courts refused the claim of the claimant for breach of confidence involving his idea for a nightclub. It was held that to attain the status of confidential information an idea must:

▨ contain some significant element of originality;

- be clearly identifiable (as an idea of the confider);

- be of potential commercial attractiveness; and

- be sufficiently well developed to be capable of actual realisation.

In *De Maudsley v Palumbo*, the idea had first been raised at a supper party where the claimant communicated his ideas for a nightclub, which he claimed had a number of novel features. The claimant claimed that the defendants were subsequently in breach by opening a 'Ministry of Sound' club along such lines without his permission.

Personal secrets

However, while the courts may be taking a more restrictive approach to confidential information in employment or business contexts, different considerations may apply in cases involving personal privacy. In *Barrymore v Newsgroup Newspapers Ltd* [1997] (a case which involved the actor Michael Barrymore seeking to restrain release of information about his personal life, from a former sexual partner, to tabloid newspapers), it was held that common sense dictated that, when people entered into a personal relationship of this nature, it was not done for the purpose of publication in newspapers; the information about the relationship was for those involved in such a relationship and not for some wider purposes.

Nevertheless, if a claimant has courted publicity, a claim may be rejected (see *Lennon v Newsgroup Newspapers Ltd* [1978]; *Khashoggi v Smith* [1980]). These judgments have been criticised in that they tend not to allow well known individuals the benefit of confidentiality. There is not a general right to privacy in English law; however, there is a distinction made between the 'celebrity' and the 'ordinary citizen'. Recent cases concerning this issue include *Campbell v MGN* [2004] where a tabloid published a story concerning a supermodel's sessions with Narcotics Anonymous. The case proceeded to the House of Lords which held that the pictures of the supermodel outside the door of Narcotics Anonymous and the accompanying details had overstepped the privacy boundaries. Other recent cases include *Douglas v Hello! Ltd* [2003] and *Theakston v MGN* [2002].

However, in the case of *X & Y* [2006] the High Court recognised that even where a person courts publicity, this does not give the press *carte blanche* over revealing details of all of that person's life, therefore preserving a celebrity's right to private life.

Employment

Confidentiality cases often arise in the context of terms of employment.

> ### ▶ FACCENDA CHICKEN v FOWLER [1985]
>
> Facts
>
> Faccenda Chicken had employed Fowler as a sales manager, and he used a particular system in his job. He then left the company, and set up his own business, taking several of the other employees of the company with him. There was no contractual agreement which controlled the activities of employees after they left the company. However, the company sued the sales manager to prevent the sales manager using confidential information they claimed he had obtained during his employment with them. The court dismissed the claim, because the information in question was not a trade secret and therefore not protected.
>
> This case demonstrates the boundary between protectable and non-protectable information, and therefore is important if a similar scenario is presented in an examination question. Not all information which arises from the employer/employee relationship is protected by confidentiality. Only certain information will fall into the category considered by the Court of Appeal in this case to be confidential and therefore protected.

In *Faccenda Chicken v Fowler* [1985], at issue was the right to restrain information obtained during the operation of a contract of employment. The Court of Appeal held that information could be divided into three categories:

(a) information of a general or trivial type which was not confidential;

(b) information that was the employee's 'stock in trade' – working knowledge which remains confidential while the contract of employment remains in force; this obligation ceases once employment ends and any restriction should be based on an anti-competition clause; and

(c) information that was so sensitive (for example, formulae, trade secrets) that it could never lose its designation and a duty of confidence existed whether employment had ceased or not.

Faccenda Chicken v Fowler [1985]

(a) Trivial = not protectable

(b) 'Stock in trade' = protectable during employment

(c) Trade secrets = always protected

As was identified in *Printers and Finishers Ltd v Holloway* [1965], the key test as to whether information learned by an employee is capable of protection is whether:

> . . . the information in question can fairly be regarded as a separate part of the employee's stock of knowledge which a man of ordinary intelligence and honesty would recognise to be the property of his employer, and not his own to do as he likes with.

However, *Ocular Sciences Ltd and Another v Aspect Vision Care Ltd and Others* [1997] shows that:

▨ bare assertions by employers that matters are secret or confidential will not be sufficient where an employer seeks to restrain the use of information taken away by a departing employee; and

▨ even where a claim of confidential information may succeed, the court can still refuse an injunction, effectively defeating the main purpose of bringing the claim in the first place.

In *Ocular Sciences*, the two claimants sued eight defendants for breach of confidence, procuring such a breach, breach of contract, breach of fiduciary duty, conspiracy and infringement of copyright and design rights relating to the manufacture of contact lenses.

Laddie J questioned the validity of the categorisation of information type (a) in *Faccenda Chicken*, stating 'what an employee can or cannot make available to a competitor during the period of his employment has little to do with the law of confidence', again implying that employment law principles, such as duties of good faith, are more relevant.

Laddie J considered that an ex-employee is entitled to use and put at the disposal of a new employer all acquired skill and knowledge, regardless of where he acquired it. Indeed, he recognised a public interest in an employee being able to do so in cases of dispute, and that public interests should prevail over those of the former employer.

It follows that, to succeed in an action for breach of confidence once employment ceases, the employer will have to prove that the secret is one which should never be released, whatever the circumstances 'information which, in the *Coco Engineers v Clark* sense ... is confidential'.

As was recognised by the Court of Appeal in *Lancashire Fires Ltd v SA Lyons & Co Ltd and Others* [1996], the boundaries between categories of information may be hard to detect (cited in *Ocular Sciences*).

It was held that the normal presumption was that information which employees obtained without having to memorise specific documents could be taken away by them and used to the benefit of future employers.

A bare assertion by an employer during employment that a matter is secret is not enough.

The subjective view of an employer of what constitutes a trade secret is not decisive. There has to be something that is objectively a trade secret, but which is known or ought to be known by both parties.

In *FSS Travel and Leisure Systems Ltd v Johnson* [1999], the Court of Appeal held that:

- protection could not be given to acquired skill and experience (employee 'know-how');

- protection could be claimed for identifiable objective knowledge ('trade secrets');

- the critical question is to distinguish between the two categories;

- this is a question of fact determined by all relevant evidence in a particular case;

- attention also has to be paid to the extent that the information may already be in the public domain and the likely damage to the employer's business if disclosure is made.

Recent cases concerning employees include *Campbell v Frisbee* [2002]. In *Vestergaard Frandsen AS & Anor v Bestnet Europe Ltd & Ors* [2009] EWHC 657, prior to leaving their employment, the employees/defendants who had worked with their employers to research and develop an insecticide-impregnated mosquito net, surreptitiously and with some dishonesty, embarked on a project to make a rival product: 'NetProtect' after leaving their employment. The high court held that the employees/defendants were subject to an implied duty not to disclose their ex-employers' technical trade secrets after their employment had been terminated, and were therefore liable for breach of confidence. See also the Court of Appeal decision in *MVF3 APS (formerly Vestergaard Frandsen A/S) and others v Bestnet Europe Ltd and others* [2011] EWCA Civ 424, which confirmed in part the judgment of the High Court.

THE PUBLIC INTEREST DEFENCE

The question of public interest in *Ocular Sciences* is one which has developed as an important defence in breach of confidence actions.

Since the 1960s, the courts have increasingly indicated that a claim of public interest may justify the breach of the obligation of confidence.

Several of the cases overlap with copyright infringement.

To allow the publication of confidential information, a defendant must do more than raise a bare plea of public interest – it is necessary to show a legitimate ground that it is in the public interest for the matter to be disclosed.

Both equity and the common law recognised the obligation of good faith to an employer. In *Gartside v Outram* [1856], it was stated that:

> The true doctrine is that there is no confidence as to the disclosure of an iniquity. No private obligations can dispense with that universal one that lies on every member of society to discover every design which may be formed, contrary to the laws of society, to destroy the public welfare.

Typically, it was used in cases involving the exposure of unlawful acts of an employer.

The modern law of a public interest defence is taken as commencing with the authority of *Initial Services v Putterill* [1967], where price fixing agreements contrary to law were exposed. The Court of Appeal refused to strike out a defence of public interest. Lord Denning took the view that a defence of public interest was not limited to crime or fraud, but extended to any misconduct of such a nature, whether actually committed or merely contemplated, that it ought, in the public interest, to be disclosed to others. Lord Salmon considered that what was an iniquity in 1856 might be too wide or too narrow a test to apply in 1967.

In *Frazer v Evans* [1968], Lord Denning considered that 'iniquity' was not the fundamental issue underlying the public interest, but was only an example of a new test, stating that there were some things which may be required to be disclosed in the public interest and to which no confidentiality doctrine could be applied.

The defence of public interest was raised in *Hubbard v Vosper* [1972], where the public interest was exposing the harm of quack remedies promoted by the Scientology movement, revealed by a former member of the organisation.

In *Beloff v Pressdram* [1973], the court recognised that the defence of public interest was established in law, but declined to apply it in a case involving leaked documents from the *Observer* newspaper to the satirical magazine *Private Eye*. 'Public interest' was taken to mean threats to national security, breach of law, fraud and matters medically dangerous and 'doubtless other misdeeds of similar gravity'.

The reluctance to extend the doctrine by adopting a narrow definition of public interest was based on the corresponding recognition by the courts that there is a public interest in keeping many matters secret.

The courts have had to balance these requirements in a number of cases, including the following:

- *British Steel Corp v Granada TV* [1981]: the media and the journalists who wrote for it had no immunity based on public interest protecting them from the obligation to disclose their sources of information in a court of law;

- *Malone v Metropolitan Police Comrs* [1979]: the claimant claimed that telephone tapping could result in the breach of confidential information. Breach of confidentiality in cases of telephone interception were held to be acceptable if necessary in the detection of crime;

- *Cork v McVicar* [1984]: related to potential corruption by police, it was held that this was a situation where the passing of information to the press could be justified;

- *Francome v Mirror Group Newspapers* [1984]: concerned an allegation that breach of jockey club rules should have been disclosed to the police or the jockey club. The *Daily Mirror* was not an acceptable destination for the information;

- *Lion Laboratories Ltd v Evans* [1985]: concerned the results of a laboratory test in a confidential report indicating defects in a new breathalyser.

> ### ▶ LION LABORATORIES v EVANS [1985]
>
> The defendants were ex-employees of a company that manufactured a device used to breathalyse motorists suspected of drink driving. They passed information relating to errors in this device to the national press for publication, and Lion Laboratories sought an injunction to prevent this information being published. The court accepted the argument of public interest, and allowed the information to be published.
>
> This case demonstrates the operation of the public interest defence in confidentiality, and is a good illustrator of the court weighing up the competing interests in cases such as these. Rather than allowing a blanket charter for people to breach confidentiality, this case recognised the boundaries of arguing public interest as a defence. It is therefore a good example to use when considering the two sides to an argument in such cases.

The *Lion* case was the first case to succeed that did not involve an iniquity. The Court of Appeal recognised that there was a public interest in a serious issue affecting the life of citizens and the risk of wrongful convictions based upon potentially unreliable recordings of the breathalyser. The public interest in this becoming known justified the breach of confidence.

Stephenson LJ set out the following criteria that were relevant to a court when determining an issue:

- the public may be interested in matters which are not their concern;

- the media has its own interest (as stated in *Francome*) and they are particularly vulnerable to the error of confusing the public interest with their own interest;

- the best recipient for information may not be the police or other responsible body.

In *Lion*, there was no evidence of 'iniquity' on the facts of the case, but a wider public interest could be identified in the proper administration of justice. *Malone* and *Francome* both involved allegations of an iniquity. As part of the process, the Court of Appeal confirmed that there is a strong public interest in preserving confidentiality within any business to allow it to be able to rely on its employees. The approach of the Court of Appeal is to ask whether a serious defence of public interest may succeed at trial.

Stephenson LJ held that the courts should not countenance disloyalty or breach of trust. Griffiths LJ held that the defence is not a mole's charter, and that there is often a strong case for maintaining the status quo.

In *Ocular Sciences*, a further extension of public interest was made in the employment context, in that an ex-employee was held entitled to use and put at the disposal of a new employer all acquired skill and knowledge, regardless of where he acquired it.

> **Lion Laboratories v Evans [1985]**
>
> Public interest in issue
>
> Media interest
>
> Alternative recipients
>
> = factors to be weighed in determining public interest and defence

From *Lion Laboratories v Evans* [1985] and *AG v Guardian Newspapers Ltd* [1990] the public interest defence requires a balance between two competing public interests: 'the public interest in preserving confidentiality against some other countervailing public interest which favours disclosure' (Lord Goff,

Spycatcher (1988)). After *Spycatcher* (*Observer and Guardian v UK* [1992]) the narrow definition of public interest of 'crime or fraud' has seemingly been broadened.

The public interest defence is probably the best known of the defences; however, other equitable and statutory immunities are also available. These include:

(a) Consent or authorisation (*C v C* [1946]).

(b) Freedom of expression (Art 10 of the Human Rights Act).

(c) Various other miscellaneous immunities such as where a defendant has revealed information under a court order or statutory obligation. Equity may also prevent an action where the plaintiff has not come before equity with clean hands.

DAMAGES

The action for breach of confidence must be brought for damages on a tort of conversion basis (*Seager v Copydex Ltd (No 2)* [1967]). Where non-commercial information has been disclosed, it is unlikely that a claimant will be compensated for distress.

In *Dowson v Mason Potter* [1986], the Court of Appeal considered that damages should be based on the market value arising from a presumed willing seller and willing buyer. In cases where a claimant would not have parted with the information, but instead would have retained it (for example, manufacturing formulae), loss of profits would be preferable. Also a court may award an account of profits where, although information has lost its confidentiality, a defendant is poised to gain financially by breaking earlier undertakings to respect confidentiality (*AG v Blake* [2000]).

INJUNCTIONS IN CONFIDENTIALITY

When considering interim injunctive relief, the court may apply the same approach as in defamation cases and decline the grant of an injunction if the defendant intends to justify (see *Woodward v Hutchins* [1977]). However, each case will turn on its facts and, in an action, the court will weigh the competing claims of confidence against those in favour of disclosure.

An injunction will only be granted if the confidential information can be identified with some precision (*Lock International plc v Beswick* [1987]).

Even though some claims for breach of confidence may be upheld at a trial, the courts may, nonetheless, refuse to grant an injunction as it is not awarded as of right (see *Ocular Sciences* (injunction denied)).

Shelfer v City of London Electric Lighting Co [1895] decided that relief may be denied if:

- the injury to the claimant's legal rights is small; and

- it is one which is capable of being estimated in money; and

- it is one which can be adequately compensated by a small money payment; and

- it would be oppressive to the defendant to grant an injunction.

Damages in substitution for an injunction may then be given. The court also considered the purpose of an injunction – not to stop continued flow of a wrongful benefit arising from the breach, but to prevent a continuation of the breach of confidence.

Where, because of disclosure, information has lost its confidentiality, then it is still uncertain as to whether a continuing injunction can be obtained to prevent further disclosure. In *AG v Guardian Newspapers Ltd* [1990] Lord Goff was of the opinion that it would be a misuse of injunctive relief once the information was in the public domain. Support for this position was given in *Ocular Sciences Ltd v Aspect Vision Cape Ltd* [1997]. However, in considering whether or not it was appropriate to grant an injunction with regards to confidential information which was already in the public domain, the High Court judge Arnold in *Vestergaard Frandsen AS & Anor v Bestnet Europe Ltd & Ors* [2009] EWHC 657, held that the claimants were entitled to an injunction. The court noted further that even if the 'springboard doctrine' could no longer justify the grant of an injunction for the continual use of confidential information already in the public domain, an injunction might still be granted in order to prevent the defendants from benefitting from a past misuse of confidential information,

17

notwithstanding that the information was no longer confidential. The Court of Appeal in *MVF3 APS (formerly Vestergaard Frandsen A/S) and others v Bestnet Europe Ltd and others* [2011] EWCA Civ 424, did not interfere with the judge's discretion to grant the injunction.

You should now be confident that you would be able to tick all of the boxes on the checklist at the beginning of this chapter. To check your knowledge of Confidential information why not visit the companion website and take the Multiple Choice Question test. Check your understanding of the terms and vocabulary used in this chapter with the flashcard glossary.

Patents

3

A patent is a monopoly right in an invention.

Patent law is regulated by the Patents Act (PA) 1977, although decisions under the Patents Act 1949 continue to aid interpretation. The UK is also a signatory to the European Patent Convention, incorporated into the PA 1977, which is also applicable. European and other international legislation has significant impact on UK law regarding patents. Examples include the Patent Co-operation Treaty (PCT), the Trade Related Aspects of Intellectual Property Rights 1994 (TRIPS) (provides minimum levels of protection for intellectual property rights), the Convention on Biological Diversity (CBD), and the World Intellectual Property Organisation (WIPO) Patent Law Treaty (PLT).

A grant of a patent gives a monopoly in an invention for 20 years (s 25 of the PA 1977).

Applications for patents are made to the Patents Office, under the control of the comptroller, with rights of appeal to the Patent Tribunal and the courts. The comptroller may determine questions of applications and foreign and convention patents (ss 8–12 of the PA 1977).

Section 1 of the PA 1977 sets out the requirements of a patentable invention.

An invention must meet four criteria:

(a) it must be new (novelty);

(b) there must be an inventive step;

(c) it must be capable of industrial application;

(d) it must be an invention – not involving excluded material (s 1(1) of the PA 1977).

If the application does not satisfy these conditions, a patent will not be granted. If a defendant alleged to be an infringer of the claimant's patent can prove that the claimant's patent lacks any one (or more) of these criteria, the patent will be invalid so that no infringement would have occurred.

There are two types of patentable invention:

(a) product inventions; and

(b) process inventions.

Issues of patentability may arise either in connection with the grant of a patent or in a counterclaim in infringement proceedings. In 2003 the EU took steps to create a single EU patent, a direction first proposed by the Community Patent Convention of 1975. The EU plans are hoped to take effect by 2010.

Other recent amendments to UK patent law include the 2004 Patents Act introduced to give effect to the European Patent Convention (EPC) 2000. The Directive on the Patentability of Computer-implemented Inventions Com (2002) 92 is now in force.

EXCLUSIONS FROM PATENTABILITY

A number of matters are excluded from patentability on grounds of unsuitability, the existence of other methods of intellectual property law protection, public policy and morality. These exclusions cover:

- discoveries, scientific theories, mathematical models;

- literary, dramatic, musical or artistic works;

- schemes, rules, games, computer programs;

- the presentation of information;

- methods of medical treatment;

- those which, by publication or exploitation, might result in offensive, immoral or anti-social behaviour;

- plant and animal varieties or any essential biological process for the production of animals or plants not being a microbiological process or the product of such a process.

Plants may be protected under the Plant Varieties Act 1997. Proprietary rights are granted to the breeders or discoverers of new, distinct, uniform and stable plant varieties.

Alternative intellectual property protection – excluded material	
Discoveries and theories	Confidential information
Literary and artistic works	Copyright
Computer programs	Copyright
Schemes and games and information	Copyright in expression
Medical treatment	N/A
Public policy	N/A
Plants	Plant Varieties Act (1997)
Animals	See Harvard Oncomouse (2003)

Examples

Young v Rosenthal & Co [1884]: '... an invention of an idea or mathematical formulae or anything of that sort could not be the subject of a patent.'

Medical methods and techniques of treatment of disease are not patentable, but new products such as drugs may be patentable (*Wyeth and Brother Ltd's Application and Schering AG's Application* [1985]). While the composition drug may be the subject of a patent, the instructions for taking a drug will not be patentable. However, if the instructions are incorporated in a novel manner into packaging then it may be patented (*Organon Laboratories Ltd's Application* [1970]).

A substance that has previously been patented can be patented a second time for a medical use (*Wyeth*).

A method of flying an aeroplane was not patentable in *Rolls Royce Ltd's Application* [1963].

A system for arranging navigational buoys was not patentable (*W's Application* [1914]).

New rules for the card game 'Canasta' were not patentable (*Cobianchi's Application* [1953]).

The Secretary of State for Trade and Industry may vary what may be patented (s 1(5) of the PA 1977).

COMPUTER PROGRAMS

Computer programs 'as such' are excluded from patentability. The European Patent Office (EPO) has also rejected the patenting of a mental act under the guise of a computer program (*IBM's Application* [1999]). To be patentable, the program must make a contribution to the art, which is that a technical effect is produced so that a technical problem is solved.

In *Vicom Systems Inc's Application* [1987] to the EPO, it was held that what was decisive with a computer program was what technical contribution the invention makes to the known art.

This approach has been followed in *Wang Laboratories Inc's Application* [1991], the court rejecting the claim on the basis that an existing machine with a new program did not combine to create a new computer (see *Fujitsu* [1996]).

Patent protection – computer programs

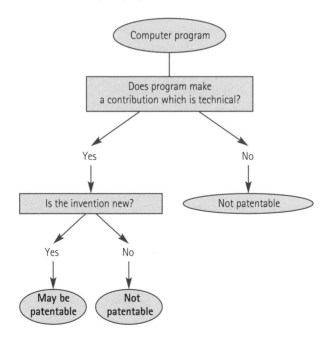

However, the EPO has ruled that computer-related inventions may be patentable in situations where they can display a technical effect and a technical character. See the *Vicom* case.

In the more recent case of *Symbian Limited v Comptroller General of Patents* [2008] (CA) the UK Court of Appeal reiterated the importance of technical contribution to prior art, as a fundamental requirement to the patentability of computer-implemented inventions.

> ▶ SYMBIAN LIMITED v COMPTROLLER GENERAL OF PATENTS
> [2008]
>
> The Comptroller General of Patents had refused Symbian's application for a patent for a computer program entitled 'Mapping dynamic link libraries in a computing device', which concerned a method of accessing data in a dynamic link library in a computing device. Dynamic Link Libraries or DLL were already known as a means of storing functions, but had an inherent weakness, which manifested whenever a new functionality was added, raising compatibility issues. Symbian's invention claimed to have solved this compatibility problem. However, the Comptroller denied patent on grounds that the invention was no more than 'a program for a computer . . . as such', and was consequently excluded as a patentable invention under section 1(2)(c) of the Patents Act, 1977 as amended. The Court of Appeal found that the differently worded 'programs for computers' employed by Article 52(2)(c) of the European Patent Convention (EPC) 2000, were not significantly different from those of Section 1(2)(c) of the Patents Act 1977, and then proceeded to apply the provisions of the former to the case.
>
> The Court of Appeal upheld the lower court's decision and held *inter alia* that Symbian's invention was not a computer program as such, that it was not excluded by the provisions of Article 52(2)(c) of the EPC, and was a patentable invention. In arriving at this decision, the Court of Appeal followed its previous decision in *Aerotel Limited v Telco Limited; Macrossan's application* [2007], where Jacob LJ laid down the following four-stage approach for determining

whether or not a computer program invention was excluded by Article 52(2)(c):

1 Properly construe the claim
2 Identify the actual contribution
3 Ask whether it falls solely within the excluded matter
4 Check whether the contribution is actually technical in nature.

In the *Symbian* case, the Court of Appeal held that stage one was not in issue. In applying stage two, the Court held that Symbian's program enabled computers to operate other programs faster than prior art operating programs, and that this was a significant contribution. With regards to stage 3, the Court held that Symbian's program did not fall solely within the excluded matter because it made computers work better. With regards to the fourth stage, the Court held that Symbian's program did make a technical contribution to the prior art.

This case illustrates the complexity involved in the interpretation of Article 52(2)(c) of the EPC, or section 1(2)(c) of the Patents Act, as the Court of Appeal itself acknowledged. The Court of Appeal's decisions in both *Aerotel* and *Symbian* cases are a clear departure from the EPO Board of Appeal's previous decisions on this issue.

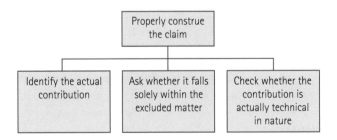

However, the outcome of the high court judgment in *Astron Clinica Ltd. & others v Comptroller General of Patents* [2009] FSR 749, would appear to have shrunk the widening gulf between the UK Patent Office and EPO on the scope of section 1(2) of the PA 1977 (Article 52(2) & (3) EPC). In the *Astron Clinica*

case, the UK Patent Office hearing officer had rejected the *Astron Clinica* patent on grounds that program claims were not allowable within the context of the requirement of the first of the four Court of Appeals tests in *Aerotel/Macrossan* that the scope of monopoly must first be considered. However, on subsequent appeal to the High Court, Mr. Justice Kitchin ruled that the practice of flatly rejecting claims to computer programs was wrong, and was not warranted by the Court of Appeals decision in *Aerotel/Macrossan*, where the issue of computer program claims never even arose. The court held further that claims to computer programs were not necessarily excluded by Article 52 EPC, and then allowed the appeal, and ordered that the application be resent to the UK-IPO for reconsideration.

Significantly, following the judgment in the *Astron Clinica* case, the UK Patent Office has re-aligned its practice with that of the EPO, which allows computer programs claims that explicitly refer to the allowable methods under section 1(2) of the PA 1977 (Article 52(2) & (3)) EPC. However, the UK patentability test must still be consistent with the *Aerotel/Macrossan* four-step tests laid down by Jacob LJ, in preference to the EPO 'technical character' test. Notably, these divergent approaches in patentability tests for computer programs, between the UK Patent Office and the EPO would appear set to continue due to the ruling of the Enlarged Board of Appeal in *G3/08* [2010] EPOR 36. The EPO President had in October 2008, referred the fractious patentability tests for computer programs to the Enlarged Board of Appeal pursuant to Article 112(1)(b) EPC. However, the enlarged Board of Appeal in *G3/08* ruled the referral inadmissible because no divergent decisions had been identified in the referral. The Enlarged Board ruled further that '... the President (of the European Patent Office) has no right of referral under Article 112(1)(b) EPC simply in order to intervene, on whatever grounds, in mere legal development if on an interpretation of the notion of "different decisions" in the sense of conflicting decisions there is no need for correction to establish legal certainty'.

PLANT VARIETIES

Although plant varieties are non-patentable, protection is given by the Plant Varieties Act 1997 and the Plant Breeders' Rights Regulations 1998 subject to the plant variety being: distinct, uniform, stable and new. The Patents and Plant Variety Rights (Compulsory Licensing) Regulations 2002 came into force on 1 March 2002, implementing Art 12 of Directive 98/44/EC.

ANIMAL VARIETIES AND BIOLOGICAL PROCESSES

Exclusion of animal varieties and essential biological processes is due to moral considerations relating to distaste for experimentation on living creatures. What has placed pressure on these exclusions is the commercial possibilities resulting from modern genetic research, eg, Dolly the cloned sheep. Currently, despite considerable debate, national and international, there is no clear agreement, notwithstanding the European Directive on the legal protection of biological inventions, on what reforms ought to be made. It may be noted that a possible way around the prohibition on essential biological processes is to patent a number of microbiological processes in the same biological field.

The provisions in relation to this area are contained within Sched A2 of the PA 1977 and Art 53(b) of the EPC, and have been specifically discussed in the Harvard Oncomouse (2003) O JEPO. The Harvard Oncomouse patent claimed a method for producing transgenic mice with a gene-based predisposition for developing cancer.

NOVELTY

To determine whether an invention is new, one considers the 'state of the art' at the priority date of the invention, that is, the date on which the patent was applied for (s 2(1) of the PA 1977) and Art 54(1) of the EPC.

The 'state of the art' is taken to include all information and material made available to the public in the UK or the rest of the world, whether in writing, orally, by use, or in any other way which is available to the public. If the invention does not form part of the state of the art, it will be new.

If a patent can be said to be anticipated – someone else has thought of it and it is in the public domain – the invention will be deprived of novelty.

A key question is disclosure – has the invention been made known to the public anywhere?

If so, the patent will probably fail for lack of novelty. But if a product or process has been kept secret, another inventor may be able to obtain a patent if he has independently reached the same result, providing all the other elements of patentability are present.

Also for prior disclosure to invalidate a patent application the disclosure must allow any member of the public 'in law and equity' to use it as he pleases (*Humpherson v Syer* [1887]). Consequently, where disclosure is made to persons placed under a duty of confidentiality, then, as they are not free in equity to make use of the disclosure, novelty will not have been broken (*Pall v Commercial Hydraulics* [1998]).

Once an invention has entered into the public domain, it cannot be patented: this is a rule of long standing (*Patterson v Gas Light and Coke and Co* [1877]).

When assessing prior disclosure an opponent is not entitled to piece together prior released documents in order to show that the invention was anticipated.

The receipt of a single specification by a patent agent in the UK was held to be a sufficient publication (*Bristol Myers Co's Application* [1969]). See diagram overleaf.

Disclosure may arise through prior publication of the invention (for example, in a relevant journal).

It is irrelevant that no one ever read or knew of the prior publication (*Japan Styrene Paper/Foam Particles* [1991]).

Suggestions that a skilled person would not read some material are also rejected – the assumption is that the notional skilled man is sufficiently interested to bother.

The document must actually disclose the invention to a competent person and reveal principles which underlie the invention to such an extent that a competent reader could take steps to reproduce the invention.

A test of novelty proposed in *General Tire and Rubber Co v Firestone* [1972] is that, if a document contains a clear description of the invention or the instructions to do or make something that would infringe the patent if carried out after the grant of the patent, then novelty will be defeated.

It must be something which falls within the claims of the patent and not simply something that might be an infringement:

> A signpost, however clear, upon the road to the patentee's invention will not suffice. The prior inventor must be clearly shown to have planted his flag at the precise destination before the patentee.

Novelty

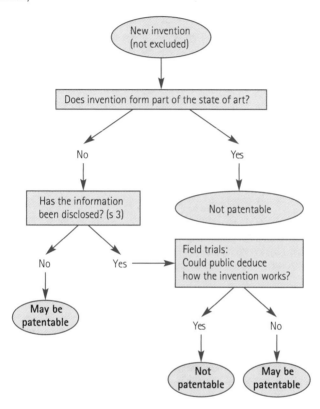

This alludes to the requirement in *General Tire and Rubber Co v Firestone* [1972] that the prior disclosure must be an enabling one so that a reader skilled in the art would be able to understand and apply the invention.

▶ **GENERAL TIRE AND RUBBER CO v FIRESTONE [1972]**

This case concerned an infringement claim on a patent for oil-extended rubber, which involved a counter-claim for validity of the patent. The court assessed the novelty of the patent by applying a test of novelty to the patent which looked at the end result the invention was attempting to achieve as the key element to be assessed for newness or novelty. In this case, the invention was adjudged to be new, and therefore the counter-claim was defeated.

This case is important in the way that the court dealt with the issue of novelty, and the concept of 'planting a flag' at the destination of the patent.

The House of Lords recently discussed this issue, and in *Synthon BV v Smithkline Beecham* [2006] decided that anticipation requires two elements: (a) prior disclosure and (b) enablement. A non-enabling disclosure (one which would not reveal the invention worked) would not destroy the novelty of the invention.

Novelty will not be destroyed by a statement that the invention will not work, nor by a disclosure which is capable of more than one interpretation. An invention can be anticipated by a single drawing, but generally more will be needed. Special rules exist for photographs (*Van der Lely (C) NV v Bamford Ltd* [1963]).

The possibility that members of the public may have seen the invention on display may be a factor which undermines novelty (*Prout v British Gas* [1992]; *Lux Traffic Controls Ltd v Pike Signals Ltd* [1993]).

Similarly, where the invention is used in public, it will fail for lack of novelty if the public may deduce how the invention works.

Circuitry of a computer is not disclosed if it is inside the computer and cannot be seen by members of the public (*Quantel v Spaceward Microsystems Ltd* [1990]).

Novelty will not arise simply where an inventor puts together a collection of old integers in a new or unusual way (*Pugh v Riley Cycle Co* [1914]). A new use for an old idea does not confer novelty (*Molins v Industrial Machinery Co Ltd* [1938]).

Disclosures do not undermine novelty for a six-month period, where:

■ the information was obtained unlawfully or in breach of confidence (for example, industrial espionage); or

■ the disclosure resulted from display by the inventor at a prescribed international exhibition and the applicant files proper notification of this (only exhibitions to educate the public occurring every 20 years fall within this); or

▨ substances and compositions involved in treatment do not form part of the state of the art.

See s 2(4) of the PA 1977 and *Kirin-Amgen v Transkaryotic Therapies* [2003].

INVENTIVE STEP

Under s 3 of the PA 1977, an invention involves an inventive step if it is not obvious to a person skilled in the art. The provisions pertaining to an inventive step are outlined in the EPC Art 52(1), the PCT Art 33(3) and TRIPS Art 27(1).

This test requires presuming a notionally skilled individual and what he would have predicted or anticipated as the next obvious stage in the development of the technology concerned. The notionally skilled person is not presumed to be imaginative or inventive himself. All factual information is relevant.

Sometimes, the notionally skilled worker is taken to be the equivalent of several workers or a research team, or deemed to possess skills of several disciplines (*Boehringer Mannheim v Genzyme* [1993]).

The notionally skilled person is assumed to read all the relevant material. Basically, the court is asking: was the invention obvious – without any inventive element or effort – or did it require more?

The notionally skilled worker is taken to have the common general knowledge of the art at the date of the invention and to be familiar with the relevant literature in the field when considering an answer to a particular problem.

A person skilled in the art is allowed to piece together (mosaic) separate items of prior art, as well as refer to other readily accessible information, as long as someone without an inventive mind could be expected to do so (*Pfizer Ltd's Patent* [2001]).

With novelty, the court is inquiring whether the invention is actually known. With inventive steps, the court has to determine whether the invention was obvious or predictable – the next step in development from the state of the art. The courts will not prevent a person from doing what is an obvious extension of existing technical knowledge, if sufficiently interested (*PLG v Ardon International* [1995]).

The nature of the problem the invention solves, its significance, how long the problem has existed, whether large numbers of people were seeking a solution and alternative solutions in the interior may all be considered when determining whether the invention is obvious (*Haberman and Another v Jackel International Ltd* [1999]).

The level of invention need only be very low. A mere scintilla of invention will be sufficient (*Parkes v Crocker* [1929]). Provided it can be detected, an inventive step will be held to be present.

Discovery by accident does not deprive an invention of patentability (*Crane v Price* [1842]). Nor is it relevant whether the inventor recognises at the time that an invention has been made (*British United Shoe Manufacturer v Fussell* [1908]). Where skilled individuals have failed to come up with an answer, it will be difficult to suggest an invention is obvious (see *Parks-Cramer v Thornton* [1966]).

The courts are wary of hindsight. In *Technograph Printed Circuits Ltd v Mills and Rockley (Electronics) Ltd* [1972], it was recognised that it is:

> . . . only because the invention has been made and has proved successful that it is possible to postulate what starting point and by what particular combination of steps the inventor could have reached his invention.

In proceedings, the court or tribunal usually relies on the evidence of expert witnesses to determine inventive step.

TESTS FOR THE INVENTIVE STEP

If the old art clearly anticipates the new, there will be no inventive step.

Various tests have been applied over the years and there are trends and fashions in judicial approach.

In *General Tire and Rubber Co v Firestone* [1972], Graham J reviewed previous authorities on obviousness, holding it relevant to ask the following questions:

(a) Does the invention have technical or commercial value?

(b) Does the invention involve a new use for an old thing? If the invention is a simple extension of a known thing, there will be no inventive step (*Reikmann v Thierry* [1897]; *Isola v Thermos* [1910]).

(c) Does the invention satisfy a long-felt want (*Longbottom v Shaw* [1891])? A history of failed attempts to reach a desired goal will be evidence of an inventive step, even if the invention is simple (*Parks-Cramer v Thornton* [1966]).

(d) Is the invention commercially successful? (Note: this may not be determinative – clever advertising or marketing might be responsible.)

(e) Have independent researchers reached the same result (*Johns Electric Ind Mfy Ltd v Mabuch 1 Motor KK* [1996])?

(f) Has the problem been identified and its solution formulated from known features? This may amount to inventiveness (the 'workmate' in *Hickman v Andrews* [1983]).

(g) How has the research area been selected? In *Re Beecham Group Ltd's (Amoxycillin) Application* [1980], it was held that the selection of a particular line or direction of enquiry can be evidence of inventive skill.

Merely because the invention is simple does not deny it patentability (*Haberman and Another v Jackel International Ltd* [1999]).

Inventive step

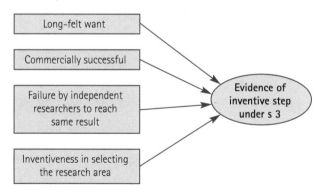

The *Windsurfer* test

The clearest modern test for determining the presence of an inventive step is the Court of Appeal's judgment in *Windsurfing International v Tabur Marine (Great Britain)* [1985], involving the navigable boom for a windsurfer.

> **WINDSURFING INTERNATIONAL v TABUR MARINE (GREAT BRITAIN) [1985]**

This case involved an infringement action where the defendants counterclaimed for the validity of the patent. The counterclaim was for revocation of the patent on the grounds that it lacked novelty, on the grounds that a 12 year old boy had used a similar windsurfer on Hayling Island in Hampshire 10 years previously. They also claimed that there was no inventiveness in the windsurfer, that it was something which was obvious, and therefore not patentable. The use, although not widely known about, had been in full view of the public, and therefore the court was satisfied that it was sufficient to anticipate the patent, and the windsurfer failed the test for obviousness that the court proposed. Therefore the infringement action was dismissed, and the patent was revoked.

The importance of this case relates to the fact that it effectively illustrates two points within patent law, firstly the point that **any** prior public knowledge of the invention will therefore make it part of the prior art, and secondly that if something does not involve inventiveness, or a 'mental leap', then it will not be patentable. It can therefore be a useful case to utilise in examination conditions. It also illustrates how the two main issues of patentability can compliment each other. Invention of the windsurfer did not involve an inventive concept, and this was illustrated also by the fact that a 12 year old boy had already used the invention in question, 10 years earlier.

The court proposed a fourfold test:

(a) identifying the inventive concept in the patent;

(b) imputing to the normally skilled, but imaginative, addressee what was common general knowledge in the state of the art;

(c) identifying the differences, if any, between the matter cited and the alleged invention;

(d) deciding whether those differences, without the benefit of hindsight, would have amounted to steps that the skilled addressee would take, or whether an inventive step was necessary.

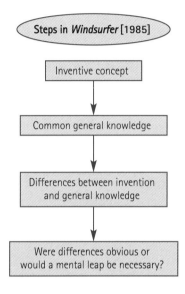

Steps in *Windsurfer* [1985]

Inventive concept

Common general knowledge

Differences between invention and general knowledge

Were differences obvious or would a mental leap be necessary?

In *Mölnycke AB v Proctor & Gamble Ltd* [1992], the *Windsurfer* steps were restated as follows:

(a) What is the inventive step?

(b) What was the state of the art at the priority date?

(c) In what respect does the step go beyond or differ from the state of the art?

(d) Would the step be obvious to a skilled man?

For recent case law concerning the use of the *Windsurfer* test, see *Sabaf SpA v MFI Furniture Centres Ltd* [2002].

Note however that the *Windsurfer* tests were slightly reworked in the Court of Appeal case of *Pozzoli Spa v BDMO SA & Anor* [2007] EWCA Civ 588 as follows: 1(a) Identify the notional 'person skilled in the art', (b) Identify the relevant common general knowledge of that person; (2) Identify the inventive concept of the claim in question or if that cannot readily be done, construe it; (3) Identify what, if any, differences exist between the matter cited as forming part of the 'state of the art' and the inventive concept of the claim or the claim as construed; and (4) viewed without any knowledge of the alleged invention as claimed, do those differences constitute steps which would have been obvious to the person skilled in the art or do they require any degree of invention? See also the Court of Appeal decision in *Schlumberger Holdings Ltd v Electromagnetic Geoservices AS* [2010] EWCA Civ 819, where the Court held that the fictional skilled addressee used for determining the inventive step could be different from the one used for ascertaining claims construction or the sufficiency of claims. See also *Conor Medsystems Incorporated v Angiotech Pharmaceuticals Inc & Another* [2008] UKHL 49, where the House of Lords overruled the Court of Appeal for not applying the correct obviousness question.

INDUSTRIAL APPLICATION

An invention must be capable of an industrial application which is satisfied if it can be made or used in any kind of industry, including agriculture, whether motivated by profit or not (*Chiron v Murex* [1996]). However, should the invention relate to an excluded category then its capability to have an industrial application will not save it (*Ward v Comptroller-General* [2000]). While strictly not required for industrial application, courts in practice tend to expect an invention to have a useful purpose, actual or potential, so as to give society a benefit in return for the grant of monopoly protection.

PROCEDURE FOR APPLYING FOR A PATENT

A patent can be obtained through either the British Patent Office or the European Patent Office, the latter being treated as if the applicant had obtained it through the UK Office.

Applications must be in English (*Rhode and Schwarz's Application* [1980]) and fulfil the requirements of s 14(2) of the PA 1977.

The application must be made by the inventor or joint inventor (s 7(2)(a) of the PA 1977).

The crucial document for an applicant is the specification, in which the invention must be clearly disclosed sufficiently for it to be performed by a person skilled in the art (s 14(3) of the PA 1977). The language must be clear enough to enable another person to be able to use the invention once the patent expires (*Edison and Swan United Electric Co v Holland* [1889]).

The specification consists of two parts:

(a) the description (which may include diagrams and technical drawings) explaining how the invention works and usually the abstract; and

(b) the claims, which cover the scope of the legal monopoly claimed by the patentee.

The wording of the claims is crucial and words and phraseology fall to be construed according to general and specific rules of interpretation.

There is no requirement to describe every possible way in which the invention is to be utilised (*Quantel v Spaceward Microsystems Ltd* [1990]).

Filing
When completed, the application must be filed with the Patent Office, under s 5(1) of the PA 1977. The priority date of the invention is the date upon which the application is filed at the Patent Office.

Preliminary examination and limited search
Section 17 is concerned with preliminary examination and search which has to be done before publication. The purpose is to ensure that the formal requirements of the PA 1977 are satisfied. It must be requested within 12 months from the filing date of the application (or an earlier application that set the priority date).

Publication
Within 18 months, the application must be published by the Patent Office allowing public inspection of the applicant's claim, as required by s 16(1).

Substantial examination and search
Within six months after publication, the applicant should request an examination and search.

The examination ensures that the patent fulfils the requirements of patentability under s 1(1).

The examiner investigates the application to the extent considered necessary (s 17(4)) and any objections to patentability must be raised with the applicant.

37

Arguments must be made within four years and six months from the initial application, unless an appeal to the Patents Court is pending.

As soon as is practicable after a patent has been granted, the comptroller must publish a notice in the *Official Journal of Patents* that the patent has been granted; a certificate is issued to the applicant. The effect of the grant puts an end to all pre-grant procedures (*ITT Industries Inc's Application* [1984]).

Monopoly period
The initial period is four years but this may be renewed for up to 20 years. As many pharmaceutical inventions (products or processes) require prolonged testing before they can be marketed, they may have an additional protective period of five years under the EU supplementary protection certificate procedure.

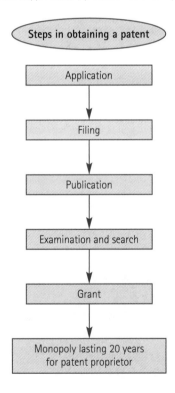

Steps in obtaining a patent

Application

Filing

Publication

Examination and search

Grant

Monopoly lasting 20 years for patent proprietor

INFRINGEMENT PROCEEDINGS

The use of or dealing with a patented invention without the permission of the proprietor will be an infringement, and the proprietor of the patent will be entitled to take action through the courts to protect his monopoly.

To amount to an infringement, the defendant must do an act which comes within the claims in the patent.

The earliest date that an infringement can occur is the date on which the application is published, normally 18 months after the priority date. But such an infringement is not actionable until the patent is granted.

Infringement of the patent consists of any of the following acts done without the consent of the proprietor of the patent, as set out in s 60 of the PA 1977:

(a) making, disposing of, offering to dispose of, importing, using or keeping a patented product;

(b) using a patented process or offering it for use in the UK;

(c) disposing of, offering to dispose of, using or importing any product obtained by using a process or keeping such a product.

'Offering to dispose' was considered in *Kalman v PCL Packaging* [1982], where it was held that disposal must include selling of an article.

Keeping a product was considered in *Smith Kline and French v Harbottle* [1980], where it was taken as meaning 'keeping in stock' for sale, rather than acting simply as a 'mere custodian or warehouseman'.

Innocent infringement will be as much an infringement as a deliberate one (*Wilbec Plastics Ltd v Wilson Dawes Ltd* [1966]).

A repairer having to make a patented part of an article will not be an infringer as the 1977 Act requires the making of the patented article (*United Wine v Screen Repair Services* [2000]).

Recent legislation
Numerous minor changes have been made to the Patents Acts, including the following:

■ Community Design (Fees) Regulations 2002: in force 1 January 2003. This Regulation indicates further progression towards the Community patent through the Office for Harmonisation in the Internal Market (OHIM).

■ Patents Act 1977 (Electronic Communications) Order 2003: this shows a move towards the usage of electronic communication.

■ The previously mentioned Patent Act 2004.

Infringing acts

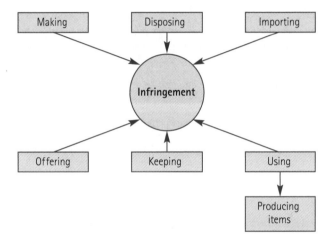

DEFENCES FOR PATENT INFRINGEMENT

A variety of defences may exist to a claim of patent infringement.

Acts which do and do not amount to infringements are set out in s 60(5) (a)–(f).

Accidental infringement

An accidental infringement, for example, where a product is manufactured by accident, will not amount to an infringement.

Stena Rederi v Irish Ferries Ltd [2003] provides a recent example of a case concerning s 60. The defendant operated a boat called the *Jonathan Swift* between Holyhead and Dublin. He unknowingly infringed the patent by entering and remaining in UK territorial waters for about three hours per visit, three or four times a day. The defendant was accused of infringing a structural boat hull patent; the defence relied upon was s 60(5)(d), which specifically excludes this as being seen as an infringing activity.

Patent infringement exemptions

The UK law regarding this area is set out in the PA 1977 and mirrored in the Community Patent Convention (CPC). Although the CPC is yet to be enacted, several European jurisdictions have used the proposed CPC to distinguish between experimental use and commercial use. US Congress has also used the distinctions in its failed attempt to codify the law on the experimental use exemption. Two general types of exemptions are found in UK patent law: the private use exemption and the experimental use exemption.

Private use

The first of the general exemptions covers uses which are deemed to be acts done privately and for purposes which are not commercial (s 60(5)(a) of the PA 1977 (see below) and also Art 27(a) of the CPC):

> An act which, apart from this subsection, would constitute an infringement of a patent for an invention shall not do so if (a) it is done privately and for purposes which are not commercial . . .

The 'and' linking the private/commercial qualifications ensures that most of the activities of governmental, educational and charitable organisations are excluded from this particular exemption. These organisations may not be commercial but they are unlikely to be private. Private use is justified on the basis that this kind of use may increase scientific knowledge and thus be socially beneficial; also, private non-commercial uses do not pose a significant threat to the patent monopoly. Where the infringing activity has both commercial and non-commercial benefits at present, the subjective intention of the user must be established. If they are deemed to be non-commercial, the defendant can rely on the exemption even if the resulting information has a commercial benefit (*SKF Laboratories v Evans Medical* [1989] and *McDonald v Graham* [1994]). This approach received significant academic criticism in the UK, the EU and the US, based on two main issues:

(a) An inquiry into the alleged intent of an individual, group of individuals, or an institution is a difficult concept to resolve.

41

(b) With regard to the legislation, intention is not deemed to be relevant to the determination of liability, the *mens rea* only playing a role in the determination of remedies: s 60(1)(a) of the Patents Act 1977.

One of the most common remedies in patent infringement cases is an award of damages (s 61(1)(c) of the PA 1977); however, in certain cases, damages will not be available where the defendant's infringement was innocent. Damages will not be awarded where the defendant proves at the date of the alleged that infringement they were not aware and had no reasonable grounds for supposing that the patent existed (s 62(1) of the PA 1977).

Experimental use
The second general exemption deals with acts done for experimental purposes relating to the subject matter of the invention and is set out in s 60(5)(b) of the PA 1977 (see below) and Art 27(b) of the CPC:

> An act which, apart from this subsection, would constitute an infringement of a patent for an invention shall not do so if (b) it is done for experimental purposes relating to the subject matter of the invention.

This exception has proved controversial in connection with patents over pharmaceutical and research tool products; however, the experimental or research exemption has traditionally protected the non-commercial activities of the research scientist in a university or governmental laboratory.

The difficulties inherent in this exemption arise from the interpretation of what is deemed to be an 'exempted experimental purpose'. This definition is resolved by analysing the commercial aspects of the research. The commercial/non-commercial criterion has a tendency to arbitrarily exclude from exemption all experimentation occurring in commercial settings. Academic commentators have suggested that there is scant policy justification for this as socially valuable research can take place. Academic institutions are increasingly marketing their research; meanwhile biotechnology and pharmaceutical industries are performing increasing amounts of basic research, which in the early stages has little commercial application.

Prior use
A prior user of an invention will have a defence (s 64 of the PA 1977).

Lack of title

A defence can be raised on the basis that the patent holder has been wrongly granted the patent and should never have obtained title.

Licence

A defendant may claim a licence to do the acts complained of by the patentee. A licence may be express or implied and may be granted orally or in writing.

Repair

A licence to repair an item may be implied where a purchaser gives a third party an item to repair.

Whether a repair has taken place is a question of fact – a new item should not be made under the guise of repair (*Solar Thompson Engineering v Barton* [1977]).

Schütz Ltd v Werit Ltd [2011] EWCA Civ 303. Schütz had a European patent on intermediate bulk containers (IBCs), which have a removable plastic inner bottle fitted into an outer protective cage. IBCs are used for a wide range of types of liquids, and the outer protective cage has a useful life span that is about five times that of the inner plastic bottles. Thus people known as 'reconditioners' would repair any damage to the cage, and replace the degraded bottles with fresh bottles from the original manufacturers. This process is known as 'rebottling'. However, if the replacement bottles are from sources other than the original manufacturers, the process is known as 'cross-bottling'. Delta, who is a reconditioner, buys discarded Schütz IBCs, removes the original damaged bottles, and replaces them with Werit bottles, and then offers the refurbished IBCs for sale in competition with Schütz. The pertinent question is whether Delta infringes Schütz's patent in the IBCs by putting a Werit bottle in Schütz cage or merely exercising its statutory right of repair?

Delivering the judgment of the Court of Appeal, Jacob LJ noted that it was an infringement to 'make a ... product which is the subject matter of the patent' under section 60(1)(a) of the PA 1977 (i.e. Art. 25 EPC), and that any perceived 'right of repair' did not exist if it led, as in this case, to the making of a new product in accordance with the patent claims.

EXHAUSTION OF RIGHTS

Section 60(4) of the PA 1977 will implement the doctrine of the exhaustion of disposal rights where a product has been put on the market with the consent of the proprietor of the patent. Where a proprietor has agreed to one disposal of a product, he is debarred from objecting from subsequent disposals.

It does not apply to goods imported from non-EC countries where there is no licence.

Frequently, a defendant in a patent suit may defend the proceedings by a so called '*Gillette* defence'. This arose from the case of *Gillette v Anglo American Trading* [1913], where the defendant claimed that the claimant's patent was invalid, because he was doing what the claimant was doing before the claimant filed the patent application. Claims that a patent fails for lack of novelty or inventive step are frequently raised by defendants in infringement proceedings.

REVOCATION OF A PATENT

A patent may be revoked under s 72 of the PA 1977.

Grounds for revocation are:

- the invention is not a patentable invention;

- the patent was granted to a person who was not entitled to be granted that patent;

- the specification of the patent does not disclose it sufficiently; and

- unallowable amendments.

Applications, which may be made by anyone (unless it is on the ground of non-entitlement where only the patent owner can apply), must normally be commenced within two years of the grant of the patent, except in cases where the registered proprietor knew he was not entitled to the grant.

These provisions do not affect revocation being sought during civil proceedings or the right of the comptroller to revoke a patent (s 72(5) and s 73 proceedings). See *Lily Icos Ltd v Pfizer Ltd* [2002].

CONSTRUCTION OF PATENT CLAIMS

Construction of patent claims is important for the patentee, as it defines the scope of the monopoly, and for others who wish to make or use similar items. Where an identical product is produced or manufactured without licence, infringement is clearly established, but problems arise when an alleged infringer produces a variant of the invention.

Here, the court has to determine whether the invention has been copied in a way which infringes the claims of the patent monopoly.

The patent must be described so as to make it clear in respect of what the patent is granted for.

From *Clark v Addie* [1877], the courts developed the 'pith and marrow' doctrine that the patent might be applied to parts of an invention (known as integers).

The pith and marrow doctrine sought to determine situations where the court considered the essential integers had been copied.

However, since the case of *Catnic Components Ltd v Hill and Smith* [1982], the courts have followed what has been termed the 'purposive approach' of examining the purpose underlying the integers in an invention, rather than applying a literal approach to interpreting the claims of a patent.

▶ CATNIC COMPONENTS LTD v HILL AND SMITH [1982]

The plaintiffs, Catnic Components, were the proprietors of a patent in respect of certain steel lintels, which were commercially successful. The defendants, Hill and Smith, produced similar steel lintels. In order to avoid infringing plaintiffs' patent, the defendants slightly varied the lintels' design by slanting the rear support member at 6–8 degrees from the vertical, in contrast to the plaintiffs' design, which was perpendicular to the base. The pertinent question was whether the new lintels made by the defendants infringed the plaintiffs' patent? The court adopted a purposive rather than a literal approach to interpreting the wordings of the claims in the plaintiff's patent, and held that the patent had been infringed. The court found that the effect of the angulation of the rear support member was negligible as regards the load bearing capacity of the lintel, and that the variation had no material effect on how the lintel worked. The court then formulated the following three questions to determine the width of a patent monopoly:

(a) Does the variant put forward have a material effect upon the way in which the invention works? If yes, the invention is outside the claim and will not infringe.

(b) If no, would the variant have been obvious to a reader skilled in the art? If no, it is outside the claim, and will not infringe.

(c) If yes, would a reader skilled in the art understand that the patentee expected strict compliance as an essential requirement of the invention? If yes, the variant is outside the claim.

The *Catnic* case is significant in that it brings the UK in line with the EPO and other European patent courts, which apply a purposive interpretation. Although the *Catnic* tests were adopted in *Improver Corp v Remington Consumer Products* [1990] (see the facts below), both the Court of Appeal and the House of Lords have recently recognised in *Kirin-Amgen v Tanskarvotic Therapies* [2003] that in some cases at least, the *Catnic* tests might not be appropriate, and that the courts should ultimately follow the Protocol to Article 69 European Patent Convention (EPC) 2000.

The purposive approach that was followed in *Improver Corp v Remington Consumer Products Ltd* [1990] developed three '*Catnic* questions' to determine the width of a patent monopoly:

(a) Does the variant put forward have a material effect upon the way in which the invention works?

   If yes, the invention is outside the claim and does not infringe.

(b) If no, would the variant have been obvious to a reader skilled in the art?

   If no, it is outside the claim.

(c) If yes, would a reader skilled in the art understand that the patentee expected strict compliance as an essential requirement of the invention?

   If yes, the variant is outside the claim.

▶ IMPROVER CORP v REMINGTON CONSUMER PRODUCTS LTD [1990]

The case concerned a hair removal device called an 'Epilady', which used a spinning coiled spring which plucked hairs when they were trapped in the spinning coils. The defendant in this case produced a device that also plucked hairs in this way, but instead of using a spring, they used a spinning rubber cylinder with v shaped grooves cut in it which trapped the hairs. The infringement action claimed that the latter device infringed the patented Epilady. In looking at the question of infringement, the court had to decide whether the allegedly infringing device overlapped with the patent for the Epilady.

This case's importance comes from the way in which the court approached the question of infringement. The court took a purposive approach to infringement using the test mentioned below. The width of scope of the patent in this case meant that the alleged infringing device fell outside the scope of the Epilady patent. The court said 'no', 'yes' and 'yes' to the 3 'Catnic questions'. This shows that when construing patent claims, it is important to note that the courts take a very narrow approach. Although the rubber cylinder did exactly the same thing as the spring, it was a slightly different approach on the same theme.

The validity of *Catnic*, as reformulated in *Improver*, as the standard test for infringement was confirmed by the Court of Appeal in *Wheatley (Davina) v Drillsafe Ltd* [2001]. The *Catnic* principle was also re-affirmed by the House of Lords in the case of *Kirin-Amgen, Inc. v Hoechst Marion Roussel Ltd* [2004] UKHL 46. The decision also enabled the construction of a claim to cover products or processes, which involved the uses of technology that was unknown at the time the claim was drafted, provided that the patent specification and claims were drafted in such a manner that a person skilled in the art would understand the description to be inclusive of the new technology.

DETERMINING OWNERSHIP

Section 7 provides that any person may apply for a patent, individually or jointly. Under s 7(2), a patent may be granted to the inventor or joint inventors or to any other person entitled by operation of law.

Section 7(3) states that the inventor is the person who devised the invention.

Section 7(2)(b) provides that a person entitled to the property in the patent can make a claim.

Property is owned as personal property (s 30 of the PA 1977) and may be leased, mortgaged, licensed, given away or passed by succession.

EMPLOYEE INVENTIONS

Where an employee, in the course of his employment, has made an invention which it was part of his duty to make, the invention and, hence, the patent belong to the employer.

Employers may obtain the benefit of a patent invented by an employee by:

▓ contractual terms;

▓ operation of equity or implied term (*Triplex Safety Glass v Scorah* [1938]);

▓ operation of s 39 of the PA 1977.

The court will take the approach laid down in *Harris' Patent* [1985] to determine ownership.

Section 39 of the PA 1977

Under s 39(1), inventions made by an employee in the course of employment belong to the employer where an invention is made:

(a) in the normal course of the normal duties; or

(b) during the course of duties where the employee was under an obligation to further his employer's interests.

With s 39(1)(a) and the normal duties of the employee, the court considers whether the employee expected to invent. (The court looks at the duties the employee is engaged to do and decides whether an invention might reasonably be expected to result.)

With s 39(1)(b), in the course of duties falling outside normal duties, the court considers whether the employee was under a special obligation to further his employer's interests at the time.

In any other situation, s 39(2) provides that the invention belongs to the employee.

The duties of the employee and the place of invention may have a crucial effect on determining the ownership of the patent (see *Electrolux Ltd v Hudson* [1977]: invention made at home by employee not employed to invent; employee entitled to patent).

In *Harris' Patent* [1985], the circumstances of the duty to invent under s 39(1)(a) referred to the invention in suit, not any invention. If an invention arises from circumstances in s 39(1)(a), it will automatically fulfil the requirement of s 39(1)(b).

In *Glasgow Health Board's Application* [1996], the court had to determine ownership of an invention made by an employee with clinical responsibilities, but no contract to conduct research. The court found that the duty to treat patients did not extend to devising new devices so to do, so the application would proceed in the name of the employee alone.

Also, in *LIFFE Administration and Management v (1) Pavel Pinkava (2) De Novo Markets Limited* [2007] EWCA Civ 217, which is the first appellate decision to interpret section 39(1)(a) of the PA 1977 in over 30 years, the Court of Appeals held that an invention relating to credit swaps belonged to the employer and not the employee, on the grounds that the employee's normal duties had evolved to cover developing credit swaps systems, of the type covered by the invention in question. See diagram overleaf.

Provision also exists for compensation for employees under ss 40–42 of the PA 1977, on application in prescribed situations where the benefit of the patent might otherwise go wholly to the employer. However, from available case law it appears that an employee, working for a large-scale employer, will find it extremely difficult to make a successful claim for compensation, as per *GEC Avionics Ltd's Patent* [1992] (see Patents Act 2004).

The law has recently been updated to make it easier for employees to gain compensation for employee inventions under ss 40–42 of the Patents Act 1977, due to the difficulty employees had in gaining compensation. Section 40(1) now states that if the patent or the invention is of outstanding benefit to the employer, then the employee can claim compensation, whereas previously it was only if the *patent* was of outstanding benefit.

The case of *Kelly and another v GE Healthcare Ltd* [2009] EWHC 181 was the first to interpret the scope of 'outstanding benefit' to the employer under section 40(1) of the PA 1977. The employee claimants: Ducan Kelly and Kwok Wai Chiu were research scientists at Amersham International Plc, which was subsequently taken over by the defendants, GE Healthcare Ltd. The claimants had contributed to the first synthesis of a compound that later formed the basis of a patented radioactive imaging agent that was commercially successful to their employers. The claimants sought an award of compensation from their employer under section 40 of the PA 1977, by claiming a share of the benefits that had accrued to their employers from the patent. Justice Floyd of the Patents Court of the Chancery Division held that the patent was of outstanding benefit to the claimants' employer, and respectively awarded Dr. Kelly and Dr. Chui £1 million and £500,000, being 3 per cent of the estimated £50 million value of the patent. The court noted that section 40 of the Patent Act was only available to an employee inventor who actually devised the invention, and not to those who merely contributed to the invention, without being joint inventors. The judge held further that 'outstanding benefits' to the employer meant 'something special' or 'out of the ordinary' and more than 'substantial', 'significant' or 'good', and something that transcended what would normally be expected from paid duties. The court held further that it must be just to make a compensatory award, and that although employees were not obliged to prove a loss or the expenditure of effort and skill beyond the scope of duty, those were factors that could be taken into consideration in determining the size of a compensatory award under section 41 the PA 1977.

Out of patient (s 39)

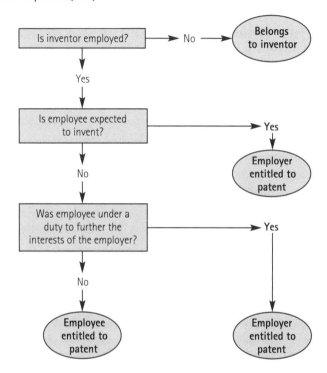

REMEDIES

Remedies in a patent infringement case are injunctions, declarations and damages, with account of profits in the alternative.

If a defendant can prove that he was not aware and had no reasonable grounds for supposing that a patent existed, then neither account of profits nor damages will be available. An article marked 'patented' will not in itself mean that innocence cannot be pleaded, but where the patent number is given then this defence will no longer be available.

Injunctions may be used to restrain potential or actual infringements (*Shoe Machinery & Co Ltd v Cutlan* [1896]).

DAMAGES IN PATENT ACTIONS

Damages in patent actions may be assessed in a number of ways.

One factor is whether the claimant would have manufactured his or her invention or process, or would have granted licences to third parties (*Pneumatic Tyre Co v Puncture Proof Pneumatic Tyre Co* [1899]).

The court may take into consideration the number of infringing articles and multiply by the sum payable under a licence (*Meters Ltd v Metropolitan Gas Meters* [1911]).

In *Watson Laidlow & Co v Pott Cassells and Williamson* [1914], the court held that the measure of damages was the amount of profit that the claimant could have made minus the sales obtained by the defendant. What may also be claimed are consequential losses, but as with any indirect loss these may be difficult to prove.

In *Catnic Components v Hill and Smith* [1982], the claimant was awarded the loss of manufacturing profits on the assumption that most of the sales of the disputed lintels would have been made by them, but not when lintels were sold in mixed packages with other products.

In *Gerber Garment Technology v Lectra Systems* [1995], the scope for awards of damages was extended to allow the claimant to recover manufacturing and marketing costs and the costs on each infringing item.

You should now be confident that you would be able to tick all of the boxes on the checklist at the beginning of this chapter. To check your knowledge of Patents why not visit the companion website and take the Multiple Choice Question test. Check your understanding of the terms and vocabulary used in this chapter with the flashcard glossary.

Copyright

4

UK copyright law is governed by Part 1 of the Copyright, Designs and Patents Act (CDPA) 1988, as amended.

The Copyright Acts of 1911 and 1956 continue to be of limited effect in certain specific instances set out in the schedules to the CDPA 1988.

INTERNATIONAL AGREEMENTS

The CDPA 1988 must also be seen in the context of Directives from the EC that are starting a process of copyright harmonisation in the Community and a number of important international agreements.

The most significant of these are as follows.

The Berne Convention
This protects the rights of authors of literary and artistic works, giving owners of rights in one Convention country the same as those in another.

The Rome Convention
This affords national protection to performers, record producers and broadcasting organisations.

The Universal Copyright Convention (UCC) 1952
This adopted the © symbol and is required for copyright protection in a country that only follows the UCC.

THE NATURE OF COPYRIGHT PROTECTION

Copyright is essentially a negative right which prevents others from making copies of the work of an author.

Copyright is a partial monopoly and the law allows a number of exceptions whereby a work may be copied legitimately without infringing the rights of an author.

Section 1(1) of the CDPA 1988 states:

> Copyright is a property right which subsists in accordance with this Part in the following descriptions of work:

(a) original literary, dramatic, musical or artistic works;

(b) sound recordings, films, broadcasts or cable programmes;

(c) the typographical arrangements of published editions.

COPYRIGHT SUBSISTENCE

Copyright does not subsist in a work unless it has been:

▨ created by a qualifying person;

▨ first published in a qualifying country; or

▨ transmitted from a qualifying country.

For literary works, the work must be reduced to a material form, in writing or otherwise (s 3(2)).

Copyright does not exist in a pure idea (*Green v New Zealand Broadcasting Corp* [1989]). The recording need not be with the permission of the author in order for the copyright to come into being. Recording can produce two separate copyrights, as in *Walter v Lane* [1900], in which a reported speech was both copyright of the speaker and the newspaper journalist who wrote it down.

A work will qualify for copyright protection if it is published in the UK or in a country to which the Act extends (s 155(1)).

Publication of a work means, under s 175(1), issuing copies of the work in question to the public. This must satisfy a reasonableness test (s 175(5)).

If a work is sold and distributed free, that is sufficient to constitute issue to the public (*British Northrop Ltd v Texteam Blackburn Ltd* [1974]). But a mere exposure or a distribution to a small class of recipients will be insufficient (*Infabrics Ltd v Jaytex Shirt Co Ltd* [1980]).

The public performance of a literary, dramatic or musical work is not publication (s 175(4)(a)(i)), nor is an artistic work published by virtue of it being exhibited.

ORIGINALITY

In order to be protected, a work must fulfil the s 1 requirement of originality. This is in the sense that the work must 'originate' from an author as its source and creator (that is, it is not copied).

In the case of *University of London Press v University Tutorial Press* [1916], it was stated:

> ... the word 'original' does not in this connection mean that the work must be the expression of inventive or original thought ... but that it should originate from the author.

In *Macmillan v Cooper* [1923], it was held that there was no need for an author 'to impart to the product some quality or character which the raw material did not possess' – a compilation of pre-existing works will still attract copyright providing that the compiler exercised 'selection, judgment and experience' or 'labour, skill and capital'. However, if no more than trifling additions and corrections are made to an existing work, it will not be sufficient to attract copyright protection anew (*Hedderwick v Griffin* [1841]; *Thomas v Turner* [1886]), nor will a mere reprint of the earlier work (*Hogg v Toye & Co* [1935]).

Nonetheless, some work, skill or effort is required, even if subject matter is mundane or banal (see *Independent Television Publications v Time Out* [1984]).

If the work is not entirely novel to an author, then the question will be whether or not sufficient embellishment has been made in order to produce a new work.

In *Ibcos Computers Ltd v Barclays Mercantile Highland Finance* [1994], Jacob J stated that a fresh copyright could arise each time a modification to a computer program was made. The issue was not affected by the fact that an original work embodied elements that could only be achieved in a number of ways.

In *Sawkins v Hyperion Records Ltd* [2005] 1 WLR 3281, the issue for determination was whether a new performing editions of four of the works of late Lalande, a composer at the courts of Louis XIV and Louis XV, sufficiently met the originality requirement under section 3 CDPA 1988, to have been infringed by Hyperion Records, who produced a CD featuring the performances of the four performing editions? It was in evidence that Sawkins spent a total of 300 hours and made over 3000 editorial interventions on the work. The Court of Appeal held that the effort, skill and time that Sawkins spent in making the performing editions was sufficient to make them 'original', even though they were based on the scores of musical works composed by Lalande, and Sawkins had made no new music as such.

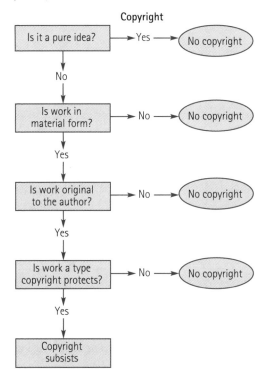

NO COPYRIGHT EXISTS IN IDEAS

No copyright exists in ideas or in very simple images unless accompanied by its expression (*Kenrick v Lawrence* [1890]).

Note, however, the decision in *Mirage Productions v Counter-Feat Clothing* [1991], but remember that this was an interlocutory decision.

No copyright exists in news until the subject matter is recorded in material work (*Walter v Steinkopff* [1892]).

No copyright exists in historical incidents or themes (*Harman Pictures NV v Osborne* [1967]).

NO COPYRIGHT IN HISTORICAL INCIDENTS OR THEMES

No copyright exists in historical incidents or themes (*Baigent & Leigh v Random House* [2007] EWCA Civ 247).

It should be recognised that it is not the *information*, but the *expression* thereof which attracts copyright protection.

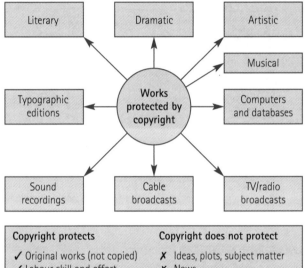

Copyright protects	Copyright does not protect
✓ Original works (not copied)	✗ Ideas, plots, subject matter
✓ Labour skill and effort of author	✗ News
✓ The expression of information by author	✗ Very simple works
	✗ Information itself

Author's source material

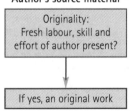

Originality:
Fresh labour, skill and
effort of author present?

↓

If yes, an original work

PRIMARY WORKS

Section 3 covers literary, dramatic and musical works, as follows:

> ... 'literary work' means any work, other than a dramatic or musical work, which is written, spoken or sung and accordingly includes:
>
> (a) a table or compilation; and
>
> (b) a computer program;
>
> 'dramatic work' includes a work of dance or mime; and 'musical work' means a work consisting of music, exclusive of any words or action intended to be sung, spoken or performed with the music.

Original literary works (s 3) covers literary works which are written, spoken or sung and excludes dramatic or musical works. Literary works include tables and compilations, computer programmes and preparatory design material.

See also the Copyright (Computer Programs) Regulations 1992 on computer programs. Under the Copyright Act 1956 and s 1 of the Copyright (Computer Software) Amendment Act 1985, a computer program was considered a literary work and proceedings would lie to prevent reproduction of the program in a machine readable form (see *Thrustcode Ltd v WW Computing Ltd* [1983]). Computer databases are also included as literary works – see the Database Directive 1996 and the Copyright and Rights in Databases Regulations 1997.

Literary works

The majority of reported copyright cases have involved literary works of one description or another.

The CDPA 1988 uses the word 'work', which requires the creation to have involved labour, skill and effort.

There is no requirement for a work to have literary merit in the sense of being aesthetically pleasing, pleasurable, entertaining, educational or contributing to the common good (*Exxon Corp v Exxon Insurance* [1982]).

The concept of a literary work in the copyright context is a wide one and has been held to include compilations. Article 2.5 of the Berne Convention requires the exercise of skill in the selection of materials in a compilation.

> ▶ **BBC AND INDEPENDENT TELEVISION PUBLICATIONS v TIME OUT [1984]**
>
> This case concerned a claim by BBC and ITP for copyright in the television schedule information for the terrestrial channels. *Time Out* had published a whole week's schedules in their magazine. The television companies claimed such information belonged to them and was protected by copyright because skill, labour and effort had gone into their creation. The court agreed, and their infringement action against *Time Out* magazine was upheld.
>
> This case demonstrates that something does not have to be particularly exciting or thought of as a great work in order to be protected by copyright, and therefore originality is shown merely by the fact that the work has not been copied from others. The situation has changed with regards to TV listings magazine due to the interference of European competition law, but the principle still stands.

However, UK law is flexible – copyright protection will subsist in telephone directories, lists of broadcasts and transmissions (see, for example, *BBC and Independent Television Publications v Time Out* [1984]). Effort and labour is involved even though the subject matter is mundane.

Examples
- Private letters: *British Oxygen v Liquid Air* [1925].
- *Donoghue v Allied Newspapers Ltd* [1938].
- Examination papers: *University of London Press v University Tutorial Press* [1916].
- List of starting prices for horse races: *Odhams Press Ltd v London and Provincial Sporting News Agency* [1936].
- Lists of football matches: *Football League Ltd v Littlewoods Pools Ltd* [1959].
- A trade catalogue: *Collis v Cater* [1898].

Notes taken by a student in a lecture will attract copyright protection. There may be copyright in notes made on a noncopyright text if knowledge, skill and taste are exercised in their preparation, notwithstanding the same material is to be found in standard texts or that the notes consist of quotations from non-copyright sources: *Moffat v Gill* [1901].

Literary efforts denied copyright protection include:

▨ single invented words (*Exxon Corp v Exxon Insurance Ltd* [1982]);

▨ titles (*Francis Day and Hunter v Twentieth Century Fox Corp Ltd* [1940] – 'Man who broke the bank in Monte Carlo'; *Rose v Information Services Ltd* [1987]);

▨ telegraph codes (*Anderson v Lieber Code* [1917]);

▨ an advertisement consisting of four commonplace sentences (*Kirk v Fleming* [1928]).

Dramatic works

A dramatic work must be capable of being performed (*Green v New Zealand Broadcasting Corp* [1989]). It can include a work of dance or mime, as distinct from a musical work, and must be recorded in writing or some other form by s 3(2) (see above). The Court of Appeal has defined a dramatic work as any work of action, with or without words or music, that is capable of being performed before an audience (*Norowzian v Arts Ltd (No 2)* [2000]).

The detailed plot of a dramatic work can be protected (*Vane v Famous Players* [1923–28]).

Artistic works

An artistic work is defined under s 4 as including:

(1) (a) a graphic work, photograph, sculpture or collage, irrespective of artistic merit;
    (b) a work of architecture being a building or a model for a building;
    (c) a work of artistic craftsmanship.

(2) In this Part, 'building' means any fixed structure, and a part of a building or a fixed structure.

Graphic work includes:

(a) any painting, drawing, diagram, map, chart or plan;
(b) any engraving, etching, lithograph, woodcut or similar work.

'Photograph' means a recording of light or other radiation on any medium on which an image is produced or from which an image may be by any means produced which is not part of a film.

'Sculpture' includes a cast or model. The work has to be three-dimensional.

Artistic craftsmanship is covered but some degree of artistic quality is needed (see *Hensher (George) v Restawhile Upholstery (Lancs)* [1976]).

In *British Leyland v Armstrong* [1986], concerning the manufacture of exhaust pipes, the co-ordinates of a pipe could be included in the definition of artistic work. To prevent monopolies based on copyright in common industrial shapes, copyright protection has been removed for articles lacking artistic merit where copying takes the form of making an article to a design or copying an article made to a design (s 51 of the CDPA 1988).

Copyright has been held to subsist in three simple circles (*Solar Thompson Engineering Co Ltd v Barton* [1977]).

Artistic works lacking permanence may not be the subject of copyright protection (*Merchandising Corp of America v Harpbond* [1983], concerning the face paint of Adam Ant, the musician).

Musical works
Musical works are judged by the effect on the ear (*Austin v Columbia Gramophone Co Ltd* [1917–23]). There is no requirement of quality, only that the work, which may only be a few notes or chords, was original and that expression is satisfied (*Lawson v Dundas* [1985]).

Under the CDPA 1988, a musical work is one consisting exclusively of musical notes, regardless of any words or actions intended to be sung, spoken or performed with it (ss 1(1)(a), 2(1)).

A separate copyright will exist in the words of a song as a literary work as well as the notes of the music as a musical work (*Redwood Music v B Feldman & Co Ltd* [1979]).

Sound recordings
Sound recordings consist of reproducible recordings of sounds, or literary, dramatic and musical works (s 5(1)) from which sounds reproducing the work or part of it may be produced.

No copyright will subsist in a sound recording that is itself a copy of another recording.

Computer programs

Computer programs are treated as the equivalent of literary works (*Thrustcode Ltd v WW Computing Ltd* [1983]), enacted into law by the Copyright (Computer Software) Act 1985.

Computer programs are specifically protected by s 3(1)(b) of the CDPA 1988, with preparatory designs protected under s 3(1)(c).

The Copyright (Computer Programs) Regulations 1992 came into effect on 1 January 1993, amending the CDPA 1988, and applies to computer programs whenever created, following EC Directive 91/250/EEC. Regulation 4 inserts new ss 50A, 50B and 50C into the CDPA 1988.

FILMS

'Film' means a recording on any medium (including celluloid, video and digital recording), providing a moving image can be produced from it (s 5B(1) of the CDPA 1988). Film relates to the recording that is made, not to the subject matter that is depicted on the film or video. A soundtrack to a film is taken to be part of the film itself.

Under the 1911 Act, films were only protected as dramatic works or a series of photographs (Sched 1, para 7 of the CDPA 1988). The 1956 Act protected films made after 1 June 1957. The CDPA 1988 applies to films made after 1 August 1989. The producer and principal director are taken to be the author (s 9(2) of the 1988 Act, substituted by SI 1996/2967).

TYPOGRAPHICAL EDITIONS

Under s 8, the typographical arrangement of published editions and any part thereof are protected for literary, dramatic or musical works, unless it is a reproduction of a previous typographical arrangement.

ANONYMOUS AND PSEUDONYMOUS WORKS

Works with no identifiable author are subject to protection by virtue of s 9 of the CDPA 1988.

CROWN AND PARLIAMENTARY COPYRIGHT

The Crown and Parliament have copyright in works made by officials and servants in the course of their duties.

WHAT IS PROTECTED

Copyright protects the original skill, labour and effort of an author (*Ladbroke (Football) Ltd v William Hill* [1964]). See also *Sawkins v Hyperion Records Ltd* [2005] 1 WLR 3281.

It is not the information itself but the use that the author has made of it in the creation of an original work.

If a person has unfairly appropriated the labour, skill or effort of an author by copying either an original work or a substantial part of one, an action will lie against the infringer.

Determining whether a person has made an unfair appropriation of the work of another is considered in terms of what use the person copying has made of the work and whether he has brought fresh labour, skill and effort to the material so as to create a new original work.

In *Elanco Products v Mandops (Agrochemical Specialists) Ltd* [1979], the claimant had invented a herbicide, the patent of which had expired. The herbicide was sold with an accompanying leaflet. Buckley LJ held that the defendants were entitled to make use of information that was in the public domain but not to appropriate the claimant's skill and judgment, thus saving the cost of time and effort in acquiring their own data, eg, using the claimant's work to take a short cut.

THE QUALITY NOT QUANTITY DIVIDE

The amount of the copyright work which can be taken before infringement arises is generally quite small.

In determining whether the amount of a work which has been taken amounts to a copyright infringement, the courts have stressed that the test is more one of 'quality than quantity' (*Newspaper Licensing Agency Ltd v Marks and Spencer plc* [2001]).

In *Ladbroke (Football) Ltd v William Hill* [1964], Lord Reid stated:

> '... the question whether the defendant has copied a substantial part depends much more on the quality than the quantity of what he has taken.'

The same view was taken in *EMI v Papathanasiou* [1987] ('*Chariots of Fire*'), where the test was taken to be qualitative not quantitative – although quantity may betray quality (*LB Plastics v Swish Products* [1979]). Copying a small part of an original work could constitute infringement.

The classic enunciation of this principle was in *University of London Press v University Tutorial Press* [1916]: '... what is worth copying is worth protecting', but this is arguably too broad, and the modern approach of the courts is to have regard to the word 'substantial' in s 16(3)(a) of the CDPA 1988. However, if it is established that the two works contain similarities then it will probably be unnecessary to have to consider substantiality (*Designer Guild v Williams* [2001]).

Protected by copyright
Author's:
✓ labour
✓ skill
✓ effort
Quality not quantity
(*Ladbroke (Football) Ltd v William Hill* [1964])

In *Spelling Goldberg Productions Inc v BPC Publishing Ltd* [1981], it was held that a tiny proportion of a work could be substantial if possessing a key feature by which the whole work could be identified or recognised.

> ▶ **SPELLING GOLDBERG PRODUCTIONS INC v BPC PUBLISHING LTD [1981]**
>
> This case concerned a poster which, it was alleged, infringed the television programme 'Starsky and Hutch'. The poster had been made from a still frame from one episode of the TV show. It was contended by the makers of the poster that this was such a small

proportion of the overall copyright work, that this could therefore not be an infringement of the copyright in the work. The court held that it was an infringement due to the significance of the work that was taken, and this was to be judged in qualitative, rather than quantitative terms. The still picture taken was recognisably of the most significant aspects of the TV show, and therefore in qualitative terms an infringement.

The point that this case makes regarding infringement is important because it allows an assessment to be made of whether an actionable infringement has occurred. Often with cases of copying, there is not a question as to whether copying has occurred, but whether that is significant enough to warrant a finding of infringement. This case provides an extreme example of the quality versus quantity issue and therefore can help to illustrate this point in an examination question.

The courts do not apply a percentage basis when determining when there has been appropriation. Attempts to identify a percentage basis of an amount that may be taken are notoriously unreliable – each case will turn on its facts.

In *Sillitoe v McGraw Hill Books* [1983], 5% of a novel was a substantial appropriation.

In *Express Newspapers v Liverpool Daily Post and Echo plc* [1985], one-700th of a literary work was substantial.

In *Chapple v Thompson Magazines* [1928–35], four lines of a popular song were held not to be substantial.

However, note *Kipling v Genostan* [1917–22], where four lines of the famous poem, 'If', were held to be substantial.

In *Hawkes v Paramount Films* [1934], 20 seconds from a melody lasting four minutes were held to be substantial.

COMMON SOURCES
Copyright can be obtained in a work based upon common non-copyright sources which are in the public domain (*Pike v Nicholas* [1867]).

In *BBC and Independent Television Publications v Time Out* [1984], Whitford J stated:

> Anyone reading a copyright work based upon publicly available information is of course free to go away and, starting with the public source and from that source, to produce his own work which may correspond very closely with the work of the earlier author. What he is not entitled to do is take a short cut.

It will be a legitimate use of a text to use it as a guide to non-copyright sources (*Moffat and Paige Ltd v George Gill and Sons Ltd* [1901]).

Unoriginal parts of a book, derived from non-copyright sources, may sometimes be copied without infringement arising (*Warwick Films v Eisenger* [1969]).

REPRODUCTION OF A NON-FICTION WORK AS FICTION

Reproductions of works dealing with factual or historic subjects reproduced in fictional form can be an infringement if a substantial part is taken (*Harman Pictures v Osborne* [1967]).

Attempts to apply a percentage basis are unreliable (*Ravenscroft v Herbert* [1980]).

EXTENT OF ALTERATION

The extent of alteration may be relevant in determining infringement.

Separate copyrights will not arise where only trivial corrections or alterations are made to an existing work (*Hedderwick v Griffin* [1841]; *Thomas v Turner* [1886]).

An unlawful reproduction does not become less of an infringement 'because the reproducer has disfigured his reproduction with ignorant or foolish additions of his own' (*Caird v Sime* [1887]).

It is possible for a work to be infringing and original (*ZYX Music v King* [1995]).

The question is not simply whether a defendant has added a sufficient degree of skill or labour to create an original work, rather it is the use that has been made of the claimant's copyright work.

DETERMINING INFRINGEMENT

The approach of the courts is to take a three-stage test. In *Bowater Windows Ltd v Aspen Windows Ltd* [1999], the test was summarised as:

(a) identifying objective similarities;

(b) deciding whether similarities are the result of independent creation ('original') or copying;

(c) if copied, whether a substantial part has been taken.

There must be a causal connection between the two works, eg, the defendant's work was derived from the copyright work.

INFRINGEMENT

Tests for copying

It should be recognised that there is no tort of copying – it is where the copyright is infringed that liability arises in law (*Cantor Fitzgerald Int v Tradition (UK)* [2000]). The approach of the courts is to examine the two works for objective similarities.

If similarity is revealed between the two works, the burden of proof then shifts to the defendant to explain away the similarities (*Corelli v Gray* [1913]).

Liability arises whether copying is deliberate or unconscious (*Francis Day Hunter v Bron* [1963]).

Indirect copying will equally be an infringement of an original work (*Purefoy v Sykes Boxall* [1954]).

A reproduction of a work changing the scale of dimensions of a work may be an infringement.

A causal connection must be shown between the two works (*Francis Day Hunter v Bron* [1963]).

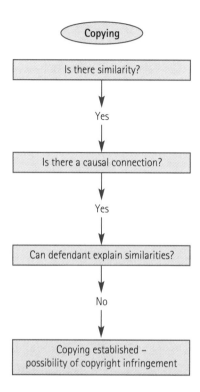

In *Billhofer Maschinenfabrik GmbH v TH Dixon and Co Ltd* [1990], it was said, *obiter*, that, when considering causal connection as to whether an alleged infringement was copied from a copyright work, it was the resemblance in essentials, the small, redundant, even mistaken elements of a copyright work which carried the greatest weight, because these were the least likely to have arisen independently.

With very simple drawings, the degree of similarity must be very close (*Politechnika Ipari Szovetkezet v Dallas Print Transfers Ltd* [1982]).

Literary works
Copyright in a book can be infringed where an undue amount of material is used, even if the language is different or the text is 'scrambled' (*Chatterton v*

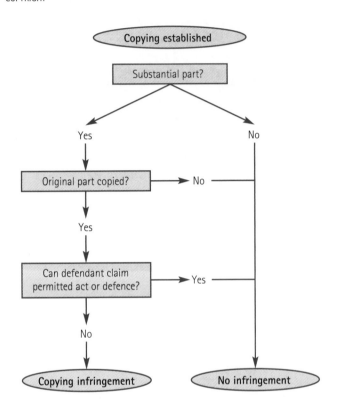

Cave [1878]; *Elanco Products Ltd v Mandops (Agrochemical Specialists) Ltd* [1980]). Again, what is protected is the labour, work, skill and effort of the author (*Cantor Fitzgerald Int v Tradition (UK)* [2000]).

Artistic works

In cases involving artistic works, the courts have looked to the resemblance to the original and whether what is copied is a significant part.

Under s 17(3) a three-dimensional copy of a two-dimensional work (and vice versa) will equal artistic copying (*King Features Syndicate v Kleeman* [1941]).

In *West v Francis* [1822], the courts stated: '... a copy is that which comes so near to the original as to give every person seeing it the idea created by the original.'

In *Spectravest Inc v Aperknit Ltd* [1988], similarity in artistic work was judged by the impression on the eye.

With a number of similar drawings of one image or character, for example, cartoon characters, the court may look at points of similarity.

Musical works

Copying of musical works is judged by the effect on the ear.

In *Stephenson v Chappell and Co Ltd* [1935], the use of identical notes constituting the melody in two songs was *prima facie* evidence of infringement.

Dramatic works

Dramatic works will not be infringed if only the bare plot has been copied (*Sutton Vane Famous Players* [1928–35]), and there will be no infringement in standard or stock scenes, since these will lack the originality of the first work (see *Dagnall v British and Dominion Film Corps Co Ltd* [1928–35]). It is an infringement to transform a non-dramatic work into a dramatic one (for example, turning an autobiographical work into a drama without permission), and vice versa, under s 21(3)(a)(ii).

Infringement of computer programs

In *Ibcos Computers Ltd v Barclays Mercantile Highland Finance* [1994], Jacob J held that the approach to take is:

(a) in what work(s) does the claimant claim copyright?;

(b) whether copyright subsisted in the relevant works;

(c) whether there had been copying;

(d) whether substantial copying had taken place – by comparison.

Proving copying requires:

(a) the defendant had access to the program;

(b) similarities between the works.

In *MS Associates v Power* [1985], it was held that, if there is only one way of expressing information, infringement may not be taken as occurring.

It will not be an infringement of a computer program to make a back-up copy (Art 5(2) of the Software Directive; s 50A of the CDPA 1988). Section 50B covers decompilations, and s 50C covers lawful users.

Screen displays may be protected as artistic works (*Atari v Phillips* [1995]).

Copying

Copyright in a work is infringed by copying the work, issuing copies of it to the public, or making an adaptation of it without licence (ss 16–18).

Reproduction in any material form will amount to an infringement of copyright (s 17). This includes storing by electronic means – for example, computers.

Under s 17(6), transient or incidental copies are infringements.

Adaptation

Section 21 of the CDPA 1988 provides that an adaptation of a literary work (with the exception of a computer program), without permission, may be an infringement. Under s 21(3), an adaptation includes:

(a) a translation;

(b) a version of a dramatic work when changed into a nondramatic one or vice versa;

(c) a version of the work conveyed by pictures (*Eskandar Nabavi v Eskandar Ltd and Shirin Guild* [2002]).

Databases

Database protection is harmonised amongst EC Member States by the Directive on the Protection of Databases (March 1996) and incorporated into domestic law by the Copyright and Rights in Databases Regulations 1997.

PRESUMPTIONS IN COPYRIGHT INFRINGEMENT

In an action for infringement of a literary, dramatic, musical or artistic work, it is presumed:

(a) that the person who is named as author is the author;

(b) that if first publication of a work qualifies it for copyright, copyright subsists and was owned at first publication by the person named as publisher;

(c) that where the author is dead or unidentifiable when the action is brought, the work was original and was first published at the date the claimant alleges (s 104).

Presumptions	
Named author	= author
or	
First publisher	= owner of copyright
Dead/anonymous author	= work is original and published at date stated

RIGHTS OF THE AUTHOR OF A COPYRIGHT WORK

If material is entitled to protection, the right vested in the copyright owner is that of preventing others from doing certain specified acts, called restricted acts.

Under s 16, the author of a work enjoys exclusive rights to:

(a) copy the work;

(b) issue copies to the public;

(c) perform, show or play the work in public;

(d) broadcast the work or include it in a cable program;

(e) make an adaptation of the work or do any of the above.

Section 16(2) provides that to do any of these acts without the authority of the author is an infringement of copyright.

Section 16(3) provides that infringement arises whether the acts are done in respect of a substantial part of the work or a whole.

Strict liability applies, even if the copier believes that he is entitled to carry out the act, but innocent belief will go to the measure of any damages.

> **Section 16: rights of author**
> Infringement – restricted acts
> Copying
> Issuing
> Performing
> Broadcasting
> Adapting

EUROPEAN COMMUNITY DIRECTIVE 2001

This Directive of May 2001 attempts to harmonise certain copyright and related rights issues as preparation for the anticipated information society – delivery of material by digital online methods. The Directive gives authors the exclusive right to authorise or to prohibit reproduction of their work. Any breach of this reproduction right will equal infringement. A similar reproduction right is given to film producers and to broadcasting organisations. Permanent and temporary digital online reproductions are caught.

The Directive also gives copyright holders a right to authorise or to prohibit the communication of their works to the public irrespective of the method of communication used.

In addition, the Directive will strengthen the position of copyright holders who use technical devices to prevent the infringement of their work. Member States will be required to have adequate legal protection to use against those who try to circumvent the use of such technology, eg, hackers of 'top-box' devices or encryption systems.

The Directive does, however, provide exceptions for temporary copies where such copies are intended only for the normal functioning of a piece of technology such as a computer, so for example, computers make copies of websites in their own memory as part of the normal function of the computer.

AUTHORSHIP

The author is the person who creates the work (s 9).

This is the person whose labour, skill and effort bring the work into existence. The author must be a British citizen or subject, or domiciled or resident in the UK (s 154(4)(b)), or in a country to which the CDPA 1988 applies.

Cummins v Bond [1927]: the person who holds the pen is the creator of the literary work unless he is simply writing down the dictated words of another (so called amanuensis).

Donoghue v Allied Newspapers Ltd [1938]: where a ghost writer has been used, the copyright belongs to the 'ghost'.

In *Wiseman v George Weidenfeld and Nicolson Ltd and Donaldson* [1985], it was held that copyright subsists with the author who puts ideas into form and development; mere supply of ideas does not generate a claim of joint ownership.

See 'Ownership of copyright' on p 81.

PERFORMING AND TRANSMISSION

With the exception of artistic works, it is an infringement to show or perform works in public without authorisation of the copyright owner. It is also an infringement to broadcast or transmit by cable (ss 19 and 20). The Performing Rights Society protects the copyright of authors by 'policing' unauthorised performances.

As to the meaning of public performance, see *Harms (Inc) Ltd v Martans Club (Ltd)* [1926] (performance in a club as a performance in public).

See also:

- *Jennings v Stephens* [1936];
- *Turner v PRS* [1943];
- *PRS v Harlequin* [1979].

The crucial issue gleaned from the above cases is whether or not the copyright owner's economic interests have been harmed.

PERFORMING RIGHTS

Performers enjoy performing rights under Part II.

These include performances before 1 August 1989, by operation of s 180(3).

Performing rights exist in the live performance of a musician, singer or actor. The permission of the performer(s) is needed before their performance may legally be exploited (s 180(1)).

SECONDARY INFRINGEMENT

Sections 22–26 of the CDPA 1988 create the concept of secondary infringement which may catch persons who knowingly enable or assist in primary infringements.

Secondary infringement occurs where a person without the licence of the owner:

- imports an infringing copy (s 22);

- possesses an infringing copy (s 23);

- sells, exhibits or distributes infringing copies (s 23);

- deals with items used for making infringing copies of specific works (s 24);

- permits premises to be used for an infringing performance (s 25);

- provides apparatus for infringing performances (s 26).

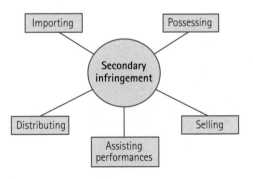

An article is defined as an infringing copy where its making is an infringement of the copyright in a work (s 27).

Knowledge, or reason to believe they are committing secondary infringement, is an essential element. Examples include: providing methods whereby infringing copies can be made, such as photocopiers; providing premises for unauthorised performances; and importing copies.

Shutting one's eyes to the obvious can be infringement (*R v Kyslant* [1934]). However, if the claimant fails to provide details of alleged infringement it may mean that the defendant will lack the necessary *mens rea* (*Vermaat v Bonenest Ltd (No 2)* [2001]).

Each act of infringement will be a separate tortious act.

A director may be liable for infringement by a firm (*Besson (AP) Ltd v Fulleon Ltd* [1986]).

In *Sony Music Entertainment (UK) Ltd v Easyinternetcafe Ltd* [2003], Easyinternetcafe had been offering a service that enabled customers to enter their premises and download music tracks onto a CD. Section 70 (recording for the purposes of time shifting) was argued, but was rejected due to the commercial use aspect. The significance of this case will be short-lived due to the implementation of the Copyright Directive into UK law.

MORAL RIGHTS

The CDPA 1988 provides rights of paternity and integrity and the right not to have works treated in a derogatory manner (ss 77–89).

The right to paternity recognises the right of the author to be identified as creator. See also *Sawkins v Hyperion Records Ltd* [2005] 1 WLR 3281, where the Court of Appeal held that failure to acknowledge Dr Sawkins' authorship in the remake of the late Lalande's musical work Hyperion Records amounted to a breach of his moral rights.

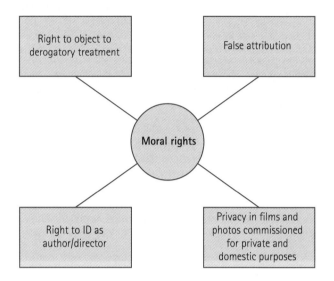

EFFECT OF COPYRIGHT PROTECTION

If material is entitled to protection, the right vested in the copyright owner is that of preventing others from doing certain specified acts, called restricted acts.

The author has exclusive rights to copy the work, issue copies to the public, perform, show or play the work in public, broadcast the work or include it in a cable programme, make an adaptation of the work or do any of the above (s 16, see p 71).

Strict liability applies, even if the copier believes that he is entitled to carry out the act, but innocent belief will go to the measure of any damages.

REPRODUCTION IN ANY MATERIAL FORM (s 17 OF THE CDPA 1988)

The copying of the work is an act restricted by the copyright in every description of a copyright work.

Copying in relation to a literary, dramatic, musical or artistic work means reproducing the work in any material form (s 17(2)).

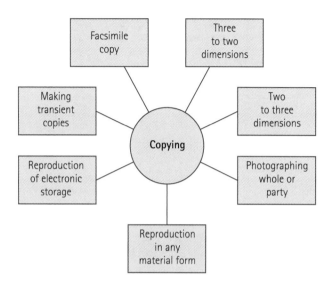

Section 17 also catches the making of a photograph of the whole or any substantial part of any image forming part of a film, broadcast or cable programme and making facsimile copies of typographical arrangements.

PERMITTED ACTS

Sections 28–76 of the CDPA 1988 provide for a wide range of circumstances in which reproduction will not be an infringement. Reproduction will be lawful providing it is done for one of the permitted reasons. (Note, also, public interest, under s 171.)

Fair dealing (ss 29–30) may mean reproduction is legitimate – the court judges the fairness of the defendant's conduct.

Fair dealing may be raised where the copying of the work is for the purposes of:

- research and private study (s 29);

- criticism or review (s 30);

- reporting current events (excluding photographs) (s 31).

Current events can include historical matters, for example, *Associated Newspapers v News Group Newspapers* [1986].

See *Beloff v Pressdram* [1973].

In *Hubbard v Vosper* [1972], Lord Denning held that fair dealing was incapable of an all-embracing definition and each case would turn on its facts.

Denning suggested the following were all relevant:

- number of quotations;

- extent of quotations;

- the use made of the extracts (is there comment, criticism or review?);

- proportion of extracts to the amount of comment.

Criticism of a work can include the ideas to be found in a work and its social and moral implications as well as style (*Pro Sieben Media AG v Carlton TV* [1999]).

> **Fair dealing**
> Private study?
> Criticism/review?
> News reporting?
> Acknowledgement?
> Is use by the defendant fair?

Short extracts from World Cup soccer games taken from BBC broadcasts and reproduced on satellite TV news broadcasts were not infringements (*British Broadcasting Corp v British Satellite Broadcasting* [1992]).

Reproduction of an entire work can conceivably amount to a fair dealing – provided that the copier is *bona fide* engaging in one of the permitted acts.

Claims of a defence of fair dealing will be scrutinised closely. In *Sillitoe v McGraw Hill Books* [1983], the defendants published extracts of books used in English literature courses in manuals for study revision. The claimed defence of fair dealing failed as the copying was for their own commercial purposes, not for those of the students who might legitimately have raised such a defence.

If the work is unpublished or confidential then the fair dealing defence fails (*Hyde Park Residence Ltd v Yelland* [2001]).

There is a public interest in free speech (*Kennard v Lewis* [1983]), but the claim will not automatically be a justification (*Associated Newspapers v News Group plc* [1986]).

The fair dealing defence can now only be made out where there has been a sufficient acknowledgement under s 178, the fairness being derived from the fact that the party copying is not seeking to assert rights of ownership over the work.

How has the defendant used the work?	
Fair uses	*Unfair uses*
✓ As a guide to earlier sources	✗ To save time, labour and effort
✓ News reporting	✗ Merely reproducing
✓ Criticism or review	✗ Reproduction without acknowledgement
✓ Private research and study	✗ Exploitation or profit without licence
✓ Other permitted uses	✗ Malicious motive act
✓ Public interest	✗ To compete against the claimant's work

Acknowledgement involves the 'act of recognising the position or claims of a person' (*Sillitoe v McGraw Hill Books* [1983]).

Displaying a company logo may be sufficient acknowledgement (*Pro Sieben Media AG v Carlton TV* [1999]).

Permitted acts

Private study or research .... s 29
Criticism, review, news reporting .... s 30
Incidental inclusion... s 31
Educational, libraries and archives............................ ss 32–44
Collective licensing .... s 35
Public administration .... ss 45–50
Judicial proceedings .... s 45

Section 29: Research and private study – an example of the effects of SI 2003 No 2498

An exception exists to cover the use of a copyright work used for non-commercial research or private study if the work is 'accompanied by a sufficient acknowledgement' unless 'this would be impossible for reasons of practicality or otherwise'. It also states that fair dealing with a literary, dramatic, musical or artistic work for the purposes of private study does not infringe any copyright within the work. The EU's Information Society Directive implemented in the Copyright and Related Rights Regulations 2003 (SI 2003 No 2498, in force 31 October 2003) clarified that copying for the purposes of commercial research is not fair dealing and amended s 29 of the CDPA 1988. The 2003 Regulations have restricted the scope of this section in two main ways:

(a) They have reduced the research element of s 29, limiting it to research for non-commercial purposes. Private businesses will not be able to rely on this section if the nature of the copying (not the nature of the business) is deemed to be commercially focused. It is also unclear if universities, charities and other public bodies will foul of these new reduced non-commercial copying criteria in the light of the increasing commercialisation in these sectors. Under ss 38, 39 and 43 of the CDPA 1988 a business can request a non-profit library to copy a single copy of a short extract from a copyright work such as a book. Generally this defence is very limited as a single copy of short extract is all that is permitted.

(b) They have restricted the definition of private study. This now excludes study which is used directly or indirectly for commercial purposes.

The 2003 legislation, which has led to the revision of the legal rules relating to this particular section, does not clarify or specifically define the exact nature of commercial or noncommercial purposes. The directive does, however, specify that the determination of what is commercial depends upon the purpose for which the copy is required, not the nature of the institution in which or for which the copy is made. This may allow pockets of completely non-commercial activities such as *pro bono* and charitable work to exist within profit making companies.

A speaker enjoys copyright in his words under the 1988 Act.

Section 58 provides that where a record of spoken words is made, in writing or otherwise, for the purposes of:

(a) reporting current events; or

(b) broadcasting or including in a cable programme service the whole or part of a work,

(c) it is not an infringement of any copyright in the words of a literary work to use the record or material taken from it, or to copy the record, or any such material, provided certain conditions are met.

The qualifying conditions under s 58 are very important and will not justify use of a record without express permission.

Section 58(2) provides:

(a) the record must be a direct record;

(b) the making of the record was not prohibited by the speaker and, where copyright already existed, it did not infringe that copyright;

(c) the record is not of a type prohibited by the speaker (so called 'off the record').

OWNERSHIP OF COPYRIGHT

Section 11 of the CDPA 1988 provides that copyright normally belongs to the person who created the work – 'the author'. In the case of sound recordings and films, the author is deemed to be the person responsible for making the arrangements for the sound or film recording (s 9(2)).

Note that physical possession of the work, for example, original manuscript, photograph, etc, does not entitle one to the copyright in the work. For example, a person may leave the physical expression of an original work in their will – but this does not necessarily mean that the beneficiary will have the copyright to it (see *Re Dickens* [1935] – manuscripts written by Charles Dickens did not confer the copyright).

Section 9 is subject to s 11 of the CDPA 1988, which provides that where a person creates a work under a contract of employment, then the ownership will lie with the employer, subject to any contractual terms in the contract of employment (with special provision for the Crown (s 11(3))).

In *Byrne v Statist* [1914], B was employed in the editorial office of *The Financial Times*. He was able to speak Portuguese and, along with two others, was asked by the paper to quote his terms for making a translation of a speech in Portuguese.

B was selected for the translation, which he did in his spare time. It was held that the copyright remained with him, not with the paper, because translation was not part of his normal duties.

In *Stephenson, Jordan and Harrison Ltd v Macdonald and Evans* [1952], the claimants were a firm of management consultants. H, an ex-employee, wrote a book on management consultancy. The claimants claimed to be entitled to the copyright in it, since it was based on notes prepared by H whilst assigned on duties. The Court of Appeal held that the employers were the owners of the copyright in that section of the book.

The employers were unable to assert copyright in the section of the book which was based upon three public lectures which H had given, even though the text had been typed by the claimants' staff. It was held that, as H had not received extra remuneration for lecturing, lectures were not part of his duties as an employee; the court stated that the lectures represented services supplied from which the company gained publicity. Copyright vested in the employee.

In *Beloff v Pressdram* [1973], an internal memo made by the claimant for the *Observer* was owned by the newspaper, the issue being whether she was employed under a contract of service or a contract for services.

Where an employer surrenders copyright, whether by accident or design, the agreement does not have to be in any particular form. A court may deduce the situation through general employment law principles and all the circumstances of the case.

Where an author is transferring copyright, actual or future, it is necessary that there is a written document. Section 90(3) provides that an assignment of copyright is not effective unless it is in writing signed by or on behalf of the assignor.

Section 91 deals with future copyright. An agreement made in relation to future copyrights again requires a signed instrument.

With future copyrights, the circumstances can be different on occasion, as with *AG v Guardian Newspapers* [1988]. The House of Lords was prepared to accept that there could be occasions where a duty of confidence or good faith was owed and copyright could be held on a constructive equitable trust for another (ex-MI5 officer holding copyright for the Crown – the *Spycatcher* case).

JOINT OWNERSHIP

Joint ownership may arise through s 10(1) of the CDPA 1988. Copyright is held by joint authors where their efforts are indistinguishable. Joint authorship does not arise where a creative work is compounded of parts that demand separate distinguishable contributions; for example, in a film or play, there may be separate copyrights for the script, music, scenery, costume design, etc. 'Ghost writers' writing up a celebrity's reminiscences remain owners of the copyright, not the celebrity (*Donoghue v Allied Newspapers Ltd* [1938]).

In *Levy v Rutley* [1871], it was held that co-authorship arises where collaborators work together in 'prosecution of a preconcerted joint design'.

Ownership of the copyright will be as tenants in common, see *Powell v Head* [1879]. Permission of both co-authors is needed to confer a licence (see *Mail Newspapers v Express Newspapers* [1987] – one author clinically dead). But one author can sue without permission of the other in case of infringement.

It is possible to assign or licence copyrights, including future copyrights, and bequeath them. Transfers must be in writing to be valid (s 92).

Duration
Copyright subsists for defined periods:

- **literary, artistic, dramatic and musical works** (the 'primary works') are protected for 70 years from the end of the calendar year in which the author died (s 12(2));

- where there are **joint authors**, copyright will last for 70 years after the death of the last surviving author (s 12(4));

- **primary works of unknown authorship (or published under a pseudonym)** enjoy protection for 70 years from the date it was made or, if during that period the work was made available to the public, 70 years from when it was so made available (s 12(3)); but note: if the author's name is discovered before the above 70 year period expires, but before the author's death, then the term is extended to the normal copyright period of the author's life plus 70 years (s 12(4));

- for **primary works that are computer-generated** the protective period is 50 years from the end of the year when the work was made (s 12(7));

- **Crown copyright in primary works** lasts for 125 years from the year in which it was made, unless it was published commercially within 75 years from the year it was made, when it will last for 50 years from the date it was commercially published (ss 163(3), 164, 165(3), 166(5));

- **parliamentary copyright** lasts for 50 years from the year in which the work was made (s 165(3));

- **films** are protected for 70 years after the last death of the principal director, screenplay author, dialogue author or the composer of music specially created for and used in the film (s 13B(2)). If the identity of the four individuals in unknown then protection is for 70 years from the year in which the film was made (s 13B(4)), unless in this period the film was made available to the public, when it becomes 70 years from the end of the year in which it was first made so available (s 13B(4));

- with **sound recordings** copyright lasts for 50 years from the end of the year in which it was made; or if it was released in that period, then it expires 50 years from its release (s 13A(2));

- **broadcasts and cable programmes** are given 50 years protection from when the broadcast was first made or the programme was first included in a cable programme service (s 14);

- for **typographical arrangements of published editions** copyright lasts for 25 years from the year of first publication (s 15);

- with **moral rights** the rights of integrity and paternity last for as long as copyright. The right to object to false attribution lasts for the author's lifetime plus 20 years.

COPYRIGHT REMEDIES

Remedies are regulated by case law and statute. Section 96 of the CDPA 1988 provides that a claimant is entitled to all such relief by way of damages, injunctions, account of profits or otherwise as are available in any other action involving the infringement of property rights.

Section 97 covers damages for copyright infringement and, in some cases, damage may be presumed.

In *Holmes v Langfier* [1903], a photographic portrait was published without permission – damage was presumed.

Innocent infringement by a defendant does not give rise to a right to damages (s 97(1) of the DPA 1988).

Additional damages may be recoverable (s 97(2)) having regard to all the circumstances, including:

- the flagrancy of the breach;

- any benefit accruing to the defendant from the infringement.

In *Nichols Advanced Systems v Rees and Oliver* [1979], Templeman J awarded damages where the defendants had received benefits and inflicted humiliation and loss and the conduct of one party had been deceitful and treacherous.

Statutory additional damages may be awarded, but only if normal damages is the other remedy that is awarded (*Redrow Homes Ltd v Bett Bros plc* [1998]).

As an alternative to damages, a claimant may elect an account of profits and seek to recover the profits which the defendant has made through the infringement.

Injunctions will lie for breaches of copyright, both interim and final injunctions at trial.

An injunction is frequently sought on the principles discussed above, pp 1–5.

STATUTORY AND POLICY INITIATIVES FOR DIGITAL COPYRIGHT PROTECTION

The challenges posed by protecting copyright works in the digital environment have precipitated a flurry of policy initiatives and statutory interventions in recent times. These range from the Digital Economy Act 2010, the Digital Britain Report of 2009, the Creative Britain Report of 2008, to the Gower Review of Intellectual Property of 2006.

The Digital Economy Act 2010 received Royal assent on 8 April 2010, and came into force on 8 June 2010. The primary objective of the Act was to deter digital copyright infringements, by facilitating the tracking and identification of persistent digital copyright infringers on the internet, and thereby stemming the tide of digital piracy and the concomitant economic losses to the British economy. The Act was arguably aimed at addressing some of the key policy ideas proposed in the Digital Britain Report, the Creative Britain Report, and the Gower Review of Intellectual Property, with regards to how best to appropriate and maximise the promise of the internet for the British economy.

However, sections 3 to 16 Digital Economy Act 2010, which *inter alia* deal with tracking down of persistent copyright infringers, and restricting or curtailing of their online experience, have proved very controversial because of their perceived non-discriminatory application to innocent internet service subscribers, potential clashes with users' online privacy, and susceptibility to abuse. Sections 17 and 18, which authorise the Secretary of State (with the prior consent of the Lord Chancellor, the Parliament and the court) to block access to a location on the internet 'from which a substantial amount of material has been, is being or is likely to be made available in infringement of copyright', or a location which 'facilitates' such behaviour, has proved equally controversial.

The Act was equally unpopular with major internet service providers, and in November 2010, TalkTalk and BT were successfully granted permission by the High Court to seek a judicial review of the Act, on grounds of lack of sufficient scrutiny and its propensity to harm citizens and businesses. The Act was equally slated by the report of the Hargreaves Review of Intellectual Property and

Growth, which was published in May 2011. (See Professor Ian Hargreaves, *Digital Opportunity: A Review of Intellectual Property and Growth* May 2011, at 93.) Given the flood of criticisms and the real threats of legal challenge, it is very likely that the Digital Economy Act 2010 would be substantially amended or repealed altogether.

You should now be confident that you would be able to tick all of the boxes on the checklist at the beginning of this chapter. To check your knowledge of Copyright why not visit the companion website and take the Multiple Choice Question test. Check your understanding of the terms and vocabulary used in this chapter with the flashcard glossary.

Passing off

5

The UK has no law of unfair competition, but the common law tort of passing off enables a trader to protect the goodwill that a business enjoys.

Goodwill is intangible – it exists in the minds of the public, thus bringing it within the ambit of intellectual property. The goodwill must be attached to a name or 'get-up' which the claimant can claim belongs exclusively to him. In a sense, passing off can be described as the law protecting unregistered trademarks.

Passing off may apply in situations where trade mark protection does not apply; where a registered trade mark exists the owner may sue in passing off as well as infringement (see s 2(2) of the Trade Marks Act 1994; *Wagamama Ltd v City Centre Restaurants* [1995]). An unincorporated association may have protectable goodwill, as well as a trader (*Artistic Upholstery Ltd v Art Forma (Furniture) Ltd* [1999]).

Passing off may also be used to protect titles of books and publications which cannot be protected through copyright.

The concept of passing off is based on the principle that a trader must not 'sell his own goods under the pretence that they are the goods of another man' (*Perry v Truefitt* [1842]) and that to do so is an actionable wrong.

As it is part of the common law, the definition of passing off is open to evolution and restatement, which can make a passing off action unpredictable.

However, the classic definition enunciated by Lord Parker in *Spalding v Gamage* [1915] that 'no person is entitled to represent his goods as another's' is still applicable.

> ### ▶ ERVEN WARNINK BV v TOWNEND & SONS (HULL) LTD [1979]
>
> The claimant's were one of a number of makers of Dutch advocaat, a traditional drink. This case concerned the accusation of passing off made by the claimant claiming that 'Keeling's Old English Advocaat' was damaging to the reputation of the Dutch product as it was of inferior quality. The English advocaat had captured part of the Dutch advocaat's market in the UK. The action was upheld, based on Lord Diplock's five-part test for passing off.

The crucial element of this case is the test for passing off provided by Lord Diplock (see below). The facts of this case provide the necessary example of where a misrepresentation may cause damage to the reputation of another, and the example supplied in this case is a straightforward one – that of an inferior product which did appear to confuse customers because of the evidence that part of the market share in that product was being taken by the English advocaat.

More recently, the essential elements of passing off were identified by Lord Diplock in *Erven Warnink BV v Townend & Sons (Hull) Ltd* [1979] (the *Advocaat* case) as:

- a misrepresentation;

- made by a trader in the course of trade;

- to his prospective customers or ultimate consumers of goods and services supplied by him;

- which is calculated to injure the business or goodwill of another trade;

- which results in damage to the business or goodwill of the trader or which is likely to do so.

Advocaat [1979]

Advocaat [1979]

Course of trade

Misrepresentation

Actionable passing off

Injury to goodwill

Customer

Damage

In *Reckitt and Coleman Products v Borden Inc* [1990] (the *Jif Lemon* case), the definition of passing off was reduced to three elements by Lord Oliver:

(1) goodwill or reputation attached to goods and services;
(2) PASSING OFF a misrepresentation made to the public;
(3) PASSING OFF damage – actual or potential.

> ▶ **RECKITT AND COLEMAN PRODUCTS v BORDEN INC [1990]**
>
> This case concerned the Jif Lemon, a plastic lemon-shaped container filled with lemon juice. The action was brought when the defendant attempted to use a similar lemon-shaped plastic container for their product, with the producers of the Jif Lemon claiming that they had passed off their product as their own. In deciding this case, Lord Oliver reduced the previous five-part test to a three-part test, and applied it to the situation here, finding that passing off had occurred by the use of a similar shaped container by the defendant.
>
> The case was based upon the reputation of the Jif Lemon – this had for years been the only product in the market to use a plastic lemon-shaped container. Because of this, it had acquired a distinctiveness in the market, and therefore had developed goodwill which was damaged by the competing product using a confusingly similar shaped packaging. The important thing to remember in this case is that because the shape in question was a naturally-occurring one, then it was not possible to use a registered trade mark to protect the product, but it was through use that it had acquired this distinctiveness and therefore meant that the goodwill which had been acquired could be protected.

The definition in the *Jif Lemon* case has been endorsed in subsequent cases, notably *Consorzio del Proscuitto di Parma v Marks & Spencer* [1991] and *Harrods v Harrodian School* [1996].

Thus, wherever a defendant adopts or uses the name or mark of another trader in such a way that customers are deceived, an action for passing off may lie. A trader may refer to a rival's name but must do so fairly.

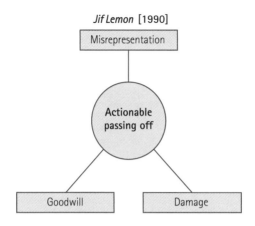

Jif Lemon [1990]

The state of mind of the defendant is irrelevant; deception may be deliberate, negligent or innocent (*Gillette v Edenwest* [1994]). The test is whether passing off is a reasonably foreseeable consequence of the deception (the *Advocaat* case).

GET-UP

The goodwill must be associated with a name or distinctive 'get-up' which acts as a badge of trade applied either to the goods or services themselves or with the name the business trades under. The name may be either real or invented (see *Hines v Winnick* [1948]).

Examples
Product name – *Bollinger v Costa Brava* [1960] ('champagne').

Advertising – *Cadbury-Schweppes Pty Ltd v Pub Squash Co Pty Ltd* [1981].

Colours – *Hoffman La Roche v DDSA Pharmaceuticals* [1969].

Packaging – *William Edge and Sons v William Nicolls and Sons* [1911] ('Dolly blue' washing powder).

Shapes – *John Haig and Co v Forth Blending Co* [1953].

Initials and combinations of letters may acquire a goodwill – see *Du Cros v Gold* [1912] and *IDW Superstores v Duncan Harris* [1975].

Titles – *Mothercare UK Ltd v Penguin Books Ltd* [1987].

In *Office Cleaning Services*, it was held that, in the case of trade names, the courts do not readily assume confusion between one trader and another where commonplace names or descriptive terms are used. This means that the name or get-up must be distinctive. However, with invented or fancy words, the risk of confusion and deception will be assumed much more readily.

It does not matter that the public do not know the precise identity of the trader, provided they associate the name or get-up with particular goods coming from a particular source (see, for example, *Birmingham Vinegar Brewery Co v Powell* [1897] (concerning 'Yorkshire relish')).

GOODWILL

In *IRC v Muller* [1901], it was stated that 'goodwill is the attractive force which brings customers in'.

In a passing off action, it is necessary to establish that the name or get-up of the goods has acquired a reputation, and trading for a limited period may be sufficient to confer goodwill.

Goodwill may attach to one trader or to a number of them collectively (*Vine Products Ltd v Mackenzie and Co Ltd* [1969]), but the larger the number of those sharing goodwill, the harder it may be to establish distinctiveness in the public mind.

Goodwill may be geographically limited (*Bernadin et Cie v Pavilion Properties Ltd* [1967]; *Guardian Media Group v Associated Newspapers Ltd* [2000]). *Associated News Ltd v Express Newspapers* [2003] where it was held that a reputation of goodwill in Birmingham is different from that found in London.

It may be possible to obtain an injunction in the UK, even though the trade takes place abroad (see *Maxim's Ltd v Dye* [1978]).

Goodwill may attach to a business even if operating only for a short time (*Stannard v Reay* [1967]). On occasion, it has even been held to exist with pre-launch activities (see *Colgate Palmolive v Markwell Finance* [1989]). Recent case law includes cases relating to international dimensions provided by the internet. In *Readmans Ltd's Application* (luxor) [2002] it was held that the existence of an internet site accessible from the UK does not give rise to goodwill.

Note: where a claimant has no goodwill in the UK, and is therefore unable to sustain a passing off action, s 56 of the Trade Marks Act 1994 may be helpful. This gives protection to well known trade marks whether or not there is goodwill in the UK.

Goodwill – attractive force bringing customers in

Must be:
✓ associated with name or 'get-up'

May be:
✓ geographically limited
✓ limited in time
✓ singular or collective

THE MISREPRESENTATION – WHO IS TO BE DECEIVED?

In a passing off case, it must be shown that customers or potential customers are likely to be deceived.

Any special features of target customers will be considered:

▨ *White v Asian Trading Organisation* [1964] (language barriers relevant);

▨ *William Edge and Sons v William Nicolls and Sons* [1911] (the *Dolly Blue* case: 'washerwomen, cottagers and other persons in humble station');

▨ *Hodgkinson & Corby Ltd v Wards Mobility* [1994] (astute health care professionals).

There is no need to prove that anyone has actually been deceived (*Bourne Swan v Edgar* [1903]).

If the defendant has set out to deceive, the law usually concludes he has succeeded (see *Slazenger v Feltham* [1889]). See also *Irvine v Talksport* [2002].

CONFUSION

Mere confusion or the likelihood of confusion is normally not enough to amount to misrepresentation – it is necessary for a customer or potential customers to be deceived (*Marcus Publishing v Hutton Wild* [1990]). See also *My Kinda Town (t/a Chicago Ribshack) v Dr Pepper's Store* [1983]. Therefore, confusion cannot automatically be asserted just because names or get-up are identical. The issue is whether the relevant public would be sufficiently confused (*Arsenal Football Club v Matthew Reed* [2001]).

However, in *Chelsea Man v Chelsea Girl* [1987], it was held that damage could take a number of forms, including confusion between two businesses experienced by traders and customers.

COMMON FIELD OF ACTIVITY

McCulloch v Lewis A May (Produce Distributors) Ltd [1947]: the claim failed, as the claimant (a children's entertainer) had no common field of commercial activity with a breakfast cereal manufacturer.

In *Wombles Ltd v Wombles Skips* [1977], there was no likelihood of confusion between the owners of goodwill in children's characters and metal rubbish skips produced by the defendant.

In *Lego v Lemelstrich* [1983], although there was no common field of activity (between a child's toy plastic brick and plastic irrigation equipment), there was a risk of damaging association and loss of licensing opportunity. Here the Lego name was an extremely well-known one.

However, in recent years, there has been a retreat away from the common field of activity doctrine, as in *Harrods v Harrodian School* [1996]. The Court of Appeal rejected a claim that the use of the name by the defendants at an educational establishment would cause such damage to the reputation of the well-known store and that 'to be known for one thing is not the same as to be known for everything'. Also, a strict requirement for a common field of activity seems to conflict with s 5(3) of the Trade Marks Act 1994 which should weaken its support.

PERSONAL NAMES

The law allows some degree of freedom for a trader to conduct business under his own name, though this right was curtailed in the 20th century:

▓ *Turton v Turton* [1889] (natural persons could trade under their personal names and could not be restrained);

▓ *Marengo v The Daily Sketch* [1948]:

> ... a man must be allowed to trade under his own name and, if some confusion results, that is a lesser evil than that a man should be deprived of ... a natural and inherent right.

The right to use one's own name

Rodgers (Joseph) and Sons v WN Rodgers [1924] imposed qualifications as follows:

▓ the person's full name must be used;

▓ the use must be honest;

▓ nothing must be done to amount to deception;

▓ the name must not be applied to goods.

In *Parker Knoll v Knoll International* [1962], it was held that, if goods are marked with a personal name and there is a likelihood of deception, no defence will lie.

There is no defence for using abbreviated names or nicknames (*Biba Group Ltd v Biba Boutique* [1980]).

> **Names**
> ✓ Full name
> ✓ Honestly used
> ✓ No deception
> ✓ Not used on goods

DAMAGE

Proof of damage is necessary in an action for passing off, unless an injunction is sought, where the likelihood of damage must be made out. A key task of the courts is to determine the types of damage of which a claimant can and cannot complain (*Hodgkinson & Corby Ltd v Wards Mobility* [1994]).

Where a trade rival adopts a name or get-up with fraudulent intent, the court may readily infer damage (*Harrods Ltd v R Harrod Ltd* [1923]) but, even if deception can be shown, it does not necessarily follow that there is recognisable damage (*Stringfellow v McCain Oven Foods (GB)* [1984]).

Registration of a famous name as a domain name on the internet amounts to passing off (*British Telecommunications plc v One in a Million Ltd*; *Virgin Enterprises Ltd v Same*; *J Sainsbury plc v Same*; *Marks & Spencer plc v Same*; *Ladbroke Group plc v Same* [1999]).

Actionable damage can be reduced to three types:

(a) diversion of custom;

(b) damage to reputation;

(c) damage by association, leading to a dilution of reputation.

DIVERSION OF CUSTOM

The most common form of damage is diversion of trade from the claimant to the defendant, with the resultant loss of sales. This covers so called classical passing off, where a defendant represents his goods as those of another, so a customer who would have bought from the claimant is deceived into buying from the defendant instead. To succeed in a claim, the parties must usually be competitors to some extent or at least engaged in the same type of industry (*Albion Motor Car Co v Albion Carriage and Motor Body Works Ltd* [1917]).

Loss of sales may be direct or indirect. In *Hoffman La Roche v DDSA Pharmaceuticals* [1969], coloured pills were sold to pharmaceutical retailers and then to the public. Although the initial purchasers were not deceived by the imitation, the fact that the colours were recognised by the public could lead to a loss of sales, even though they did not know the identity of the original manufacturer.

In *Draper v Twist* [1939], it was held that, if a defendant markets a quantity of goods which are to be taken as those of the claimant, the court will infer some loss of sales without the claimant having to prove the necessary transactions.

Where a defendant has deliberately sought to deceive the public, the court will usually assume that he has succeeded (*Lever v Bedingfield* [1898]), although each case will turn on its particular facts.

DAMAGE TO REPUTATION

Damage to reputation is a long-standing cause of action but can be hard to prove. In *Harrods Ltd v R Harrod Ltd* [1923], Warrington LJ stated: 'I think that under the word "property" may be included the trade reputation of the [claimants], and that, if tangible injury is shown to the trade reputation of the [claimants], that is enough.' Included within this can be a wide range of deceptive conduct:

- inducing a belief that one class of the claimant's goods are of another class or quality (*Teacher v Levy* [1905]);

- passing off seconds as primary manufacture (*Gillette Safety Razor Ltd v Franks* [1924]);

- selling stale goods as fresh ones (*Wiltshire United Dairy v Thomas Robinson and Sons Ltd* [1957]).

The likelihood of damage to reputation must be a serious one. In *Blazer v Yardley* [1992], an action by the claimant failed to obtain an injunction against the defendants who were well known manufacturers of perfume and toiletries. There was no evidence that the public would think any the worse of the claimant by the use of the well-known name 'Blazer' in such a context.

If there is no danger of the public being confused, then no action will lie (*Granada Group Ltd v Ford Motor Co Ltd* [1972]; *Miss World v James Street Productions* [1981]). In the latter case, the organisers of the Miss World contest failed to restrain the promoters of *The Alternative Miss World*, a film featuring transvestites and shown on the same night as the contest.

See also *Harrods v Harrodian School* [1996], pp 86 and 90.

DILUTION

Dilution of goodwill provides an alternative claim where there is no common field of activity between the parties, or where the use of a distinctive mark or name by the defendant is not likely to prove very detrimental to the claimant, but which will, over the years, lead to diminution of reputation, being cumulative in effect.

In *Taittinger v Albev* [1993], the manufacturers of champagne successfully restrained the emergence of English elderflower champagne. The argument that the appearance on the market of a product with such a name would erode the distinctive reputation of champagne succeeded. Similar arguments may be used in any case where a well known brand name is applied to a wide range of products, though generally these will be protected by trade marks.

In *Erven Warnink BV v Townend and Sons (Hull) Ltd* [1979], Lord Diplock held:

> In this class or case, there are ... two types of damage to be considered, direct loss of sales, illegitimate competition, and a more gradual damage to the [claimant's] business through depreciation of the reputation their goods enjoy.

Other categories of damage have been accepted:

▨ loss of licensing opportunity (*Lego v Lemelstrich* [1983]);

▨ risk of litigation (*Walter v Ashton* [1902]);

▨ confusion on part of customers and traders (*Chelsea Man v Chelsea Girl* [1987]).

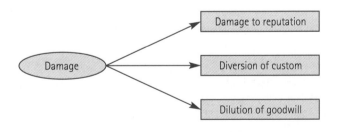

REMEDIES

As with other intellectual property rights, a successful claimant may obtain an injunction, damages or both.

▨ An account of profits is available in the alternative.

- Injunctions may be granted on conditions.

- Damages are treated in a similar way to infringement of registered trade marks. See Chapter 8.

- A delivery up order is also available.

You should now be confident that you would be able to tick all of the boxes on the checklist at the beginning of this chapter. To check your knowledge of Passing off why not visit the companion website and take the Multiple Choice Question test. Check your understanding of the terms and vocabulary used in this chapter with the flashcard glossary.

Malicious falsehood

6

An action for malicious falsehood may lie in common law for statements which damage the business reputation of another or his goods. The tort is also known as injurious falsehood or trade libel and is triable before a single judge and not before a judge and jury as in libel actions. Malicious falsehood usually has relevance where the plaintiff does not own a registered trademark.

Statements may be made orally or in writing (*Ratcliffe v Evans* [1892]) and a claimant may also plead libel as well as malicious falsehood if the facts may be construed as either (*Joyce v Sengupta* [1993]).

Elements of the tort were set out in *Royal Baking Powder Co v Wright Crossley and Co* [1901]:

(a) an untrue derogatory statement;

(b) made maliciously;

(c) resulting in special damage.

These principles were restated in *Kaye v Robertson* [1990].

▶ KAYE v ROBERTSON [1990]

This case is an example of where malicious falsehood can also be used outside the commercial sphere in protection of privacy. The three principles laid out in the *Royal Baking Powder* case were stated and applied here. Gordon Kaye was an actor who was in hospital because of an injury sustained in a car accident. Reporters from the *Sunday Sport* had gained access to his hospital room and had conducted an interview with him. They claimed that they had obtained Kaye's consent in conducting the interview, but the court applied the principles of malicious falsehood by coming to the conclusion that the claimant could not possibly have provided consent due to his medical condition, and found that the element of maliciousness was proven because it was obvious to the reporter in question that Mr Kaye was in no fit condition to give informed consent. The final element, of damage, was found through the fact that any value in Mr Kaye attempting to sell his story at a later date of his choosing once he had recovered was significantly lessened if the defendant was permitted to print the interview.

This case demonstrates an example of the three elements of malicious falsehood from the *Royal Baking Powder* case, and an example which allows students to distinguish this area from other areas such as passing off due to the fact that it is not so obviously directly concerning business reputation as such.

In *Atkins v Perrin* [1862], it was held that the court has to decide as a matter of fact:

- whether the defendant's belief was a genuine one;

- if genuine, whether it was one a reasonable man might hold.

Where a defendant honestly believes a statement is true, but it is in fact false, there will be no malice and an action will not lie. Neither will an action lie where a defendant makes a statement carelessly, but without any intention of harming the claimant (*Balden v Shorter* [1933]).

There must be an untrue statement or real disparagement which a reasonable man would take to be a serious claim (*De Beers Abrasive v International General Electric* [1975]).

If a defendant seeks to justify the statement at the interlocutory stage, no injunction will lie (*Schulke and May UK Ltd v Alkapharm UK* [1999]).

In *De Beers*, it was held that a person is entitled to puff his own goods with statements such as 'our goods are better than the claimant's'.

A defendant is not entitled to say that the claimant's goods are rubbish, unless he can establish that the goods are indeed rubbish.

Elements of malicious falsehood
- ✓ Malice
- ✓ False statement
- ✓ Damage

MALICE

◼ It must be established that the defendant acted intentionally or with reckless indifference (*McDonald's Hamburgers Ltd v Burger King (UK) Ltd* [1986]).

◼ Malice must be capable of being inferred (*British Railway Traffic and Electric Co Ltd v CRC Co Ltd and LCC* [1922]).

DAMAGE

Proof of damage is necessary to sustain a claim.

In *Dicks v Brooks* [1880], it was held that there must be sensible, appreciable damage.

Damage must be a direct and natural consequence of the words used.

In *Wilkinson v Downton* [1897], the claimant recovered costs for medical treatment for shock, following a malicious claim that her husband had been injured.

Until the enactment of the Defamation Act 1952, a claimant had to prove special damage. Heads of damage could include diminution in value, loss of particular transactions or licensing opportunities and general trade damage.

Section 3(1) of the Defamation Act 1952 provides that it is not necessary to prove special damage where:

(a) the words are published in written or permanent form and are calculated to cause pecuniary damage to the claimant; or

(b) the words are calculated to cause pecuniary loss to the claimant in respect of trade, office, calling or profession.

Recent cases include *DSG Retail v Comet group* [2002].

> You should now be confident that you would be able to tick all of the boxes on the checklist at the beginning of this chapter. To check your knowledge of Malicious falsehood why not visit the companion website and take the Multiple Choice Question test. Check your understanding of the terms and vocabulary used in this chapter with the flashcard glossary.

Character merchandising

7

The following can be used to protect character merchandise:

Defamation – use of defamatory images

Copyright – protection of the physical expression of a character

Trade marks

Passing off

The tort of appropriation of personality is recognised as existing in some jurisdictions.

English law provides a collection of rights and remedies whereby personalities, whether real or fictional, may be protected, and this involves a range of intellectual property rights.

Defamation, copyright, passing off, trade marks and malicious falsehood have all been employed on occasion to try to protect a property right deemed as existing in a character, although the English courts have been slow to recognise such rights.

DEFAMATION

At common law, a libel action could be brought to prevent defamatory statements aimed at a person.

Defamation might occur in written descriptions or in drawings or physical caricatures:

- *Monson v Tussauds* [1894]: display of an effigy in Madam Tussauds held to be libellous;

- *Tolley v JS Fry* [1931]: the reproduction of an image of an amateur golfer held to be libellous.

COPYRIGHT

Copyright has failed to protect the names of fictional characters, for example, 'Kojak' in *Taverner Rutledge v Trexapalm* [1975] and 'Wombles' in *Wombles Ltd v Wombles Skips* [1977], since names and titles are too short to constitute a work and thereby qualify for copyright protection.

Copyright has been invoked to protect the physical expression of a character, such as a cartoon character depicted in line drawings, for example, *King Features Syndicate v OM Kleeman* [1940] (the *Popeye* case). However, apart from the interlocutory decision, it does not appear to extend to the concept of a character in a literary or artistic work.

PHOTOGRAPHS

No right exists to prevent a person photographing another; a person is as free to take photographs as he is to produce a written description (*Sports and General Press Agency v Our Dogs Co Ltd* [1916]).

Certain rights to privacy in photographs are created among the forms of moral rights created under the Copyright, Designs and Patents Act (CDPA) 1988.

TRADE MARKS

An attempt to use trade mark protection, in *Re Pussy Galore* [1967], by the estate of Ian Fleming, for the names of 16 characters from the James Bond stories and for the words 'secret agent' failed, as it was not possible to show a *bona fide* intention to use the trade marks applied for.

Trade mark protection will only apply where the mark is being used in a trading context (see *British Sugar plc v James Robertson and Sons plc* [1996]).

PASSING OFF

Passing off has been used by both real and fictional personalities to try to protect their 'characters' from exploitation by others:

- *McCulloch v Lewis A May (Produce Distributors) Ltd* [1947]: 'Uncle Mac' radio – personality unable to restrain manufacturers of breakfast cereal who used his name.

- *Sim v HJ Co Ltd* [1959]: actor Alistair Sim unable to prevent an impersonation of his voice in a commercial.

- *Clark v Associated Newspapers Ltd* [1998]: politician and writer restrained a newspaper that falsely attributed spoof diaries to him.

Other cases involving fictional creations which were not successful before the English courts include:

- *Taverner Rutledge v Trexapalm* [1975]: 'Kojakpops' lollipops could not be restrained by image owners – different field of activity.

- *Lyngstad v Annabas* [1977]: pictures of Abba pop group could be used on T-shirts against wishes of owners.

▓ *Wombles Ltd v Wombles Skips* [1977]: no passing off in using the word 'Wombles' on rubbish skips.

Cases in other jurisdictions protecting fictional characters have been more successful. See:

▓ *Pacific Dunlop Ltd v Hogan* [1989] and *Hogan v Koala Dundee* [1991]: 'Crocodile Dundee'.

▓ *Children's Television Workshop Inc v Woolworths* [1981]: 'Muppet' characters.

In the UK, the decision in *Mirage Productions v Counter-Feat Clothing* [1991] (concerning 'Ninja Turtles') recognised that licensing of characters was a recognised business practice known to the public and that harm to the goodwill which existed in the claimant's turtles could be caused if unlicensed merchandise entered the market.

It therefore follows that both of the general elements of passing off must be established, together with proof that specific damage may result to the owners of the image from wrongful exploitation of the image.

▶ MIRAGE PRODUCTIONS v COUNTER-FEAT CLOTHING [1991]

The defendants in this case had applied images of the popular cartoon characters, the 'Teenage Mutant Ninja Turtles' to clothing products, without the permission of the creators of these characters. They were sued by the claimants for passing off, and the test developed under the *Warninks* case and the *Jif Lemon* case (see pp 84–6) were applied here. The court found in favour of the claimants, concluding that passing off had occurred.

The action was based upon the fact that the public were aware that where such characters were used on merchandise such as this, that it was usually because a licence from the creators had been obtained. The damage would therefore be in the image being portrayed, and not in a trading reputation as in passing off cases. This case is therefore an important example of the application of passing off to this particular area.

Passing off as a means of protection in character merchandising
Elements of passing off (see *Erven Warnink v Townend* [1979]; *Reckitt and Coleman Products v Borden Inc* [1990]) + Damage resulting to image or its exploitation

Character merchandising

No separate tort of
appropriation of personality

But

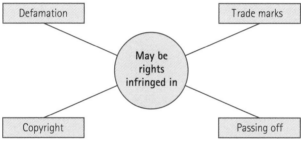

You should now be confident that you would be able to tick all of the boxes on the checklist at the beginning of this chapter. To check your knowledge of Character merchandising why not visit the companion website and take the Multiple Choice Question test. Check your understanding of the terms and vocabulary used in this chapter with the flashcard glossary.

Registered trade marks

8

Registered trade marks guarantee the origin of goods and services.

Originally developed in the 19th century, and now contained in the Trade Marks Act (TMA) 1994, the trade mark registration system protects the rights attaching to a mark in a way which the passing off cannot ensure because of the unpredictability of common law actions. Rights in passing off are expressly preserved by the TMA 1994.

The TMA 1994 implements Council Directive 89/104/EEC, makes provision in connection with the Community Trade Mark (Council Regulation (EC) 40/94) and gives effect to the Madrid Protocol for the Registration of Marks Internationally. The Act operates in the context of the 'Community' trade mark registration system, which came into effect on 1 April 1996.

The TMA 1994 replaces the Trade Marks Act 1938, but the courts have shown that they will continue to apply case law which arose under the 1938 Act and earlier trade marks legislation.

Restrictions on what may be registered are relaxed by the TMA 1994, allowing almost any identifier which distinguishes a business, and which is a feature that the public recognises as distinctive of the business, to be registered, if capable of graphic representation.

Included would be:

■ letter/numeral combinations (real or invented);

■ logo marks and business names;

■ designs;

■ designs of vehicles;

■ shapes (subject to s 3(2));

■ colours;

■ liveries or shop facades;

■ sound patterns.

A trade mark takes the form of personal property (s 22). It may be bought, sold or leased or licensed by agreement. Licensing provisions exist under ss 28–31 of the Act allowing a licensee to bring proceedings in specified circumstances.

Licences do not have to be in writing. A recent case has explored the registration of olfactory marks: *Ralf Siekmann v Deutsches Patent und Markenamt* [2002]. See also *KWS Saat AG v OHIM* [2002], where a trade mark over seed colour applied to the Office for the Harmonisation of the Internal Market.

Trade mark law has been updated specifically in relation to registration by the Trade Mark Rules 2000. Alongside this legislation various statutory instruments have been introduced in 2004. They include the Community Trade Mark (Amendment) Regulations 2004 and the Trade Marks (Amendment) Rules 2004. Recent case law includes *Arsenal Football Club plc v Reed* [2003], *R v Johnstone* [2003] and *Reed Employment v Reed Elsevier* [2004].

ADVANTAGES OF REGISTRATION

The advantages of registering trade marks include:

▓ greater protection to a mark – no need to prove elements of passing off and reputation;

▓ legal proceedings and dealings are simplified, for example, registration = title;

▓ some disputes may be resolved by the Trade Marks registrar (saving time and expense in litigation – although parties may be represented before the registrar);

▓ a registered mark is protected nationally (and now also within the EU if a Community trade mark), whereas passing off actions may only apply locally;

▓ both consumers and traders benefit from a system of registration which places limits on what constitutes a trade mark;

▓ prevention by a registered trade mark proprietor of goods that he initially sold into one EU State from being imported into another EU State (*Levi Strauss and Co and Another v Tesco Stores Ltd and Another* [2001]).

Proceedings cannot be brought for unregistered marks, though rights of passing off are expressly preserved (s 2(2)). Parties may sue in the alternative.

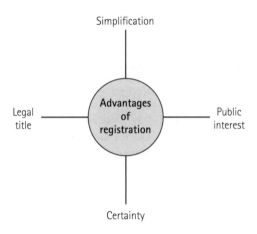

Simplification

Legal title — Advantages of registration — Public interest

Certainty

REGISTRATION

The system protects any sign which may be capable of being represented graphically (s 1(1)). The scope of what constituted graphical representation was tested in the landmark case of *Sieckmann v German Patent Office* (2002, case C-273/00), where the European Court of Justice interpreted the meaning of graphical representation of non-conventional trademarks under Article 2 of the European Trade Marks Directive 89/104/EEC (section 1(1) Trade Marks Act 1994). The main issue for determination was whether methyl cinnamate scent, a chemical formula, which the applicant described 'as balsamically fruity with a slight hint of cinnamon', was capable of being represented graphically? The ECJ held as follows: (a) a physical deposit of a sample of the scent did not constitute a graphic representation, and was not sufficiently stable or durable; (b) a chemical formula depicting the methyl cinnamate scent did not represent the odour of a substance and was neither sufficiently intelligible nor sufficiently clear and precise; and (c) the written description of the scent was not sufficiently clear, precise and objective, and therefore incapable of registration as a trade mark.

The register system is maintained by the Patent Office and is under the control of the registrar.

An application must contain a request for registration, details of the applicant, a statement of the goods and/or services to which the mark is to be applied and a representation of the mark, which means reproduction in graphical form, within a box, 8 cm × 8 cm.

Under the Trade Mark Rules 1994, 42 categories of goods and services are listed for which a trade mark may be registered. Frequently, registration may be sought for more than one category.

The registrar conducts a search of existing marks (s 37(2)) and examines whether the proposed mark meets the criteria prescribed by law for the application.

For a sign to be capable of distinguishing for the purposes of trade mark law, the sign must indicate who the product or service came from, not merely tell the customer what it is (*Philips Electronics BV v Remington Consumer Products* [1998]).

> ### ▶ PHILIPS ELECTRONICS BV v REMINGTON CONSUMER PRODUCTS [1998]
>
> This case concerned a dispute over three-headed rotary electric razors. Philips had a trade mark which consisted of the shape of their rotary shaver, and claimed that Remington infringed this by their marketing of a similar three-headed shaver.
>
> The issue here concerned the shape that Philips claimed was their trade mark – that of the three-headed design. The court's decision here was based upon the fact that the three-headed design was necessary to achieve a technical result relating to the function of the shaver. This is an important case within this area because of the fact that even where a shape such as this may be distinctive, it may still be prohibited due to it being technical in nature, due to the fact that it may prevent competitors from entering into or competing in the market in question. This case therefore demonstrates a fairly strict approach of the European Court of Justice in dealing with the absolute grounds for refusal of registration, and is a useful example of this approach.

Certain absolute grounds exist for refusal of registration, based upon mandatory and optional grounds, laid down in Art 3(1) and (2). No other grounds may be implemented by national law to found a ground for objection to registration.

Absolute grounds include the following:

- ▣ failure to satisfy s 1(1) or s 3(1)(a) (*Philips Electronics BV v Remington Consumer Products* [1998]);

- ▣ the mark is devoid of distinctive character (*Froot Loops TM* [1998]);

- ▣ the mark consists exclusively of descriptive elements (s 3(1)(c); *Re Jeryl Lynn Trade Mark* [1999]);

- ▣ the mark has become customary within the established *bona fide* trade.

Limitations are also placed on shapes of containers (s 3(2)) (*Re Dualit Trade Mark* [1999]).

Further grounds for refusal of registration include (s 3(3)):

- ▣ marks contrary to public policy (*Re Hallelujah TM* [1976]);

- ▣ marks 'of such a nature as to deceive the public' (*Orlwoola TM* [1909]).

Section 3(5) provides grounds for refusal where the mark is a specially protected emblem, for example, Royal arms, EU flags and symbols (s 4).

Section 3(6) provides grounds for refusal in cases of bad faith (*Mickey Dees (Nightclub) TM* [1998]).

Registration will also be refused if there is a conflict with an earlier register entry or an earlier right.

Under s 5, registration will be refused if there is conflict with an earlier identical mark (s 5(1)), or if the conflict is with a similar mark for similar goods, together with the likelihood of confusion and, if the conflict is with a mark that has a reputation, if registration would be unfair or detrimental to that earlier mark (s 5(3)).

Conflict with an unregistered mark (s 5(4)(a)) or other right (s 5(4)(b)) will also prevent registration.

The applicant enjoys rights of appeal both to the trade marks registrar and to the courts.

> **To be registrable, a trade mark must:**
>
> - be capable of graphical representation;
> - be distinctive;
> - not be descriptive;
> - not be excluded under the TMA 1994.

Earlier case law will assist with the meaning of these terms; arguably, the same definitions in s 5 are applicable to the corresponding terms in s 10.

A trade mark can be kept in force indefinitely, providing registration fees are paid and there is an intention to use it (s 32).

REMOVAL OF A TRADE MARK

A trade mark may be declared invalid under s 47 and removed from the register.

The application may be made by any person and may be made to the registrar or the court (s 47(3)), unless court proceedings are already taking place.

Invalidity proceedings may remove a mark from registration for all or some of its relevant registrations (s 47(5)).

GROUNDS FOR REMOVAL

Invalidity under s 47: invalid if there is a breach of s 1, 3 or 5. See *Koninklijke Philips Electronics NV v Remington Consumer Products Ltd* [2002]. See diagram on p 118.

RIGHTS IN A TRADE MARK AND INFRINGEMENT

Section 9 of the TMA 1994 provides exclusive rights to the proprietor of the trade mark in the UK. Section 9 introduces the infringement provisions of ss 10–13 which specify rights and effects of infringement. The licensing provisions under ss 28–31 of the Act allow a licensee to bring proceedings in specified circumstances. Licences do not have to be in writing.

A mark is protected from unauthorised use, which is defined, by s 103(2), as including use otherwise than by means of a graphic representation, for example, oral representations.

Section 9 rights have effect from the date of registration of the mark (s 40(3)), which is the date of filing of the application for registration). Infringement proceedings cannot begin until registration occurs (*Origins Natural Resources Inc v Origin Clothing Ltd* [1995]).

In proceedings, the Rules of the Supreme Court (Amendment No 3) 1995 provides that, in infringement proceedings, the party against whom the claim is made may, in his defence, put in issue the validity of a mark or revocation of a mark, or raise it as a counterclaim.

The infringement section stems from Art 5 of the Directive.

Primary acts of infringement arise through use (s 10(1)) Trade Marks Act and Article 5(1) of the Directive.

In *L'Oréal SA, et al. v eBay International et al.* (case C-324/09), L'Oréal sued eBay in the High Court of Justice (England & Wales) for trademarks infringement, and for facilitating and profiting from the infringement of their trademarks by online sellers on the latter's website. The High Court then referred the case to the ECJ for its views on a number of questions of law. It was in evidence that eBay purchased L'Oréal's trademarks from search engine operators as keywords to be displayed by the said search engines in a sponsored link to eBay's website. The pertinent question was whether the display of L'Oréal's trademarks in the sponsored link to eBay's website was tantamount to a 'use' of the trademarks by eBay under Article 5(1)(a) of the Trade Marks Directives and Article 9(1)(a) of the Community Trade Marks Regulation? The ECJ held *inter alia* that the linking of L'Oréal's trademarks under the circumstances could amount to a 'use' and therefore an infringement of Article 5 of the Trade Marks Directive and Article 9 of the CTM Regulation provided the sponsored advertisement did not enable reasonably well-informed and reasonably observant internet users (or enabled them only with difficulty) to ascertain whether the goods concerned originated from the proprietor of the trade mark (L'Oréal) or from an undertaking economically linked to that proprietor or, from a third party. However, on the question of whether eBay infringed the trademarks of products sold on its website, the ECJ held that eBay did not use such trademarks under Article 5 of the Trade Marks Directive, but the sellers of goods on eBay's website would be deemed to have 'used' and thereby infringed the trademarks associated with the goods they sold on eBay's website. The ECJ held further that national courts should be able to order online retailers to take measures to end infringements but also to prevent further infringements by individual sellers.

Is mark registrable?

Secondary acts of infringement require knowledge (s 10(5)).

Under s 10(1), no evidence of confusion is needed if an identical mark is used on identical goods.

For proceedings under s 10(2), where the marks and the goods or services are identical or similar, the ambit of infringement is beyond the protection provided by the Trade Marks Act 1938.

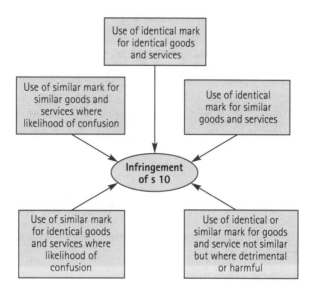

The mark or the goods need not be identical, only similar where there is a likelihood of confusion of the public. Arguably, concepts and tests of similarity relevant to s 10(2) are the same as those for s 5. See *LTJ Diffusion SA v Sadas Vertbaudet SA* [2003].

Likelihood of confusion of the public is a fundamental requirement and may be shown by evidence, but remains a separate legal test (see similarity discussion, below).

Comparison is made between the mark as registered and the alleged infringement used in relation to the particular goods and services actually concerned. Comparison is on a 'sign for sign' basis (*British Sugar plc v James Robertson and Sons plc* [1996]) and it will not assist a defendant to claim that there is no likelihood of confusion due to the distinguishing matter surrounding the mark as it is actually used.

The provision has no application where goods and services are not similar and does not overlap with s 10(3). Goods are either similar or not – there is no middle ground.

Section 10(3) provides a wholly new ground of infringement where a sign is used which is identical to or similar to a registered trade mark which has a reputation in the UK for goods or services that are not similar, for example, putting a registered trade mark for a soft drink with a reputation on a can of weedkiller. It is based on Art 5(2) of the Directive.

Under s 10(3), protection is against the dilution of a distinctive character of a mark. This is a new development in UK law, allowing an action for infringement for use of the mark on goods other than those for which the mark is registered. It is a requirement of infringement that the registered trade mark has a reputation in the UK, which is something distinct from goodwill and does not necessarily require any use in the UK.

Protection may only be limited to use in a trade mark sense, not to the use of marks (particularly word marks) in any other context (see *British Sugar plc v James Robertson and Sons plc* [1996]; *Football Association v Trebor Ltd* [1997]).

Comparative advertising is also caught to prevent one trader riding on the back of another's mark. However, note the words in s 10(6) regarding 'honest practices in industrial and commercial matters'. This provision allows, for instance, consumers to obtain information about different brands which might include the use of a trade mark. As to honest uses in business, see *Barclays Bank plc v RBS Advanta* [1996] and *Provident Financial v Halifax Building Society* [1994].

Section 10(6) requires two things for an infringement in law:

(a) use of the mark otherwise than in accordance with honest practices in industrial or commercial matters; and

(b) must without due cause take unfair advantage of, or be detrimental to, the distinctive character or repute of the trade mark.

It follows that comparative advertising may take place if fair.

Limitations are imposed by s 11 of the TMA 1994 on the scope of infringement of registered trade mark and details important circumstances where a mark is not infringed, for example, the use by a person of his own name or address (s 11(2)(a)).

A registered mark is not infringed by use in the course of trade in a particular locality of an earlier right which applies only in that locality. An earlier right means an unregistered trade mark or other sign which has been used continuously in relation to goods or services by a person or a predecessor in title, from a date preceding registration, so long as the earlier right had such goodwill as could be protected in a passing off action (s 11(3)).

Under s 16, an application for delivering up is not an infringement proceeding.

LEGITIMATE USES BY A NON-MARK HOLDER

Certain uses of a mark are permitted by a non-owner:

- a person's own name and address;

- indications of kind, quality, quantity, intended purpose, value, geographical origin, time of production or rendering, or other characteristics of goods or services;

- the mark itself, where this is necessary to indicate the intended purpose of a product or service, for example, for spare parts.

However, rights of action may still exist in passing off, which is expressly preserved.

COMMUNITY TRADE MARKS

European Council Regulation 40/94 established the Community Trade Mark registration system. The Community Trade Mark system provides protection for marks throughout the EU.

OPPOSITION

Opposition to a trade mark registration may be commenced either during the application stage or after the mark has been granted.

Any person may apply to oppose the trade mark registration.

COMPARING TRADE MARKS

Both the courts and the Trade Marks Registry may be called upon to determine whether marks are so confusing with another's registered trade mark with regard to both ss 5 and 10.

Under s 5, the registrar may refuse to register a trade mark which is identical or similar to an existing mark and there is a risk of confusion to the public.

Under s 10, infringement proceedings may be brought by the owner of a trade mark against another who uses an identical or similar mark without licence or consent.

Similarity may also be an issue in cases involving:

▓ applications for revocation or invalidity;

▓ proceedings for the restraint of use of the Royal Arms;

▓ passing off;

▓ prosecutions for unauthorised use of registered trade mark.

Each case will turn on its facts. The relevant facts for comparison are as follows:

▓ the two signs must be taken and judged by their look and sound;

▓ the goods to which the marks are applied and the nature and kind of customer must be considered;

▓ the circumstances of the trade concerned (*Kidax (Shirts) Ltd Application* [1959]) must be looked at.

Consideration is on a 'sign for sign' basis (*British Sugar plc v James Robertson and Sons plc* [1996], per Jacob J).

With words or name marks the classic test is *Pianotist* [1906], *per* Parker J:

> You must take the two words. You must consider the nature and kind of customer who would be likely to buy these goods. In fact, you must consider all the surrounding circumstances, and you must further consider what is likely to happen if each of those trade marks is used in a normal way as a trade mark for the goods of the respective owners of the mark.

If, following such consideration, the court takes the view that there is a likelihood of confusion, registration may be denied or a finding of infringement will follow.

In *Smith-Hayden and Co Ltd's Application* [1946] (*aka Re Ovax* [1946]):

... having regard to the user of the mark applied for: is the tribunal satisfied that the mark, if used in a normal or fair manner in connection with any goods covered by the registration proposed, will not reasonably be likely to cause deception and confusion amongst a substantial number of persons.

A recent case that returns to this area is *Davidoff and Cie SA and Zino Davidoff SA v Gofkid Ltd* [2002]. The question before the ECJ related to whether provisions of the First Council Directive 89/104/EEC (expressed as applying in respect of non-similar goods or services) could also apply where goods or services were similar.

See also *Arsenal Football Club plc v Reed (No 2)* [2002].

> ▶ ARSENAL FOOTBALL CLUB v REED [2003]
>
> Reed, a market stall trader, was sued by Arsenal FC for selling goods with the Arsenal logo (a registered trade mark) attached to them. Reed argued that he had not used the Arsenal logo and name in 'a trade mark sense', but instead as a badge of allegiance to the football team, as people who bought his products would do so to show that they were Arsenal supporters. The Court of Appeal, however, decided that the use did fall within the scope of 'trade mark use' under the Trade Marks Act 1994, that Reed was using the trade mark in a trade sense even if his customers may not, and therefore that Reed would be liable for infringement of the Arsenal trade mark.
>
> This case illustrates that the term 'trade mark use' will be given a wide interpretation under the Trade Marks Act. The attempt to narrow down the meaning of trade mark use in this case was unsuccessful.

Assessing similarity of marks presumed
Normal and fair use of mark
No deception
Substantial number of persons

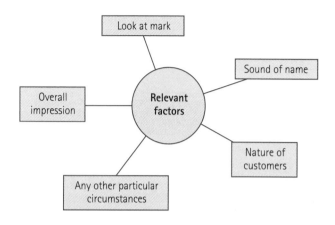

Similarity of goods:
(*Re Jellinek* [1946])

- nature and composition of goods;
- uses to which goods are put;
- trade channels through which goods are sold.

Imperfect recollection is a factor to be considered.

It is recognised that marks will rarely be seen side by side (*Reckitt and Coleman Products v Borden Inc* [1990]).

Deciding whether a mark is similar is related to but not determinative of the question of whether it is likely to confuse (see *The European v The Economist* [1996]).

When considering the impression that the two marks may have, the court ignores extraordinarily stupid or unobservant people ('moron in a hurry' from *Morning Star Co-operative Society Ltd v Express Newspapers* [1979]). In fact the 'average' consumer may be deemed to be reasonably well informed, reasonably observant and circumspect (*Lloyd Schuhfabrik Meyer v Klijsen Handel* [2000]).

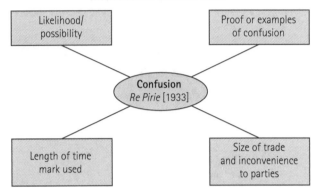

DAMAGES

Damages for trade mark infringement are similar to passing off and assessed on similar principles.

Nominal damages lie for an infringing use of a mark (*Blofield v Payne* [1833]).

The claimant may claim for the profit on every infringing item without proving that a sale occurred to a deceived consumer (*Lever v Goodwin* [1887]).

In *Alexander v Henry* [1895], damages were awarded for fraudulent use of the claimant's mark and loss of sales.

You should now be confident that you would be able to tick all of the boxes on the checklist at the beginning of this chapter. To check your knowledge of Registered trade marks why not visit the companion website and take the Multiple Choice Question test. Check your understanding of the terms and vocabulary used in this chapter with the flashcard glossary.

Design rights

9

Designs with 'eye appeal' are registrable under the Registered Designs Act 1949.

Registration is with the Patent Office following prescribed rules on application of the design right owner (s 3).

Section 1 of the Registered Designs Act 1949 as amended, defines registrable designs as being:

> . . . features of shape, configuration or ornament applied to an article by any industrial process, being features which in the finished article appeal to and are judged by the eye.

Such appeal 'is that created by the distinctiveness or shape, pattern or ornament calculated to influence the customer's choice' (*Interlego v Tyco Industries Inc* [1988]). The 'eye' is that of consumers or potential consumers (*Isaac Oren v Red Box Toy Factory* [1999]).

If there is no question of eye appeal, the design will not be registrable under s 1(3).

The EC Design Directive (98/71) provides a new design definition (Art 1): '. . . the appearance of the whole or part of a product resulting from the features of, in particular, the lines, contours, colours, shapes, textures or materials of the product itself or its ornamentation.' The law relating to registered designs has been supplemented recently by the Registered Design Regulations 2003 (SI 2003/550).

The design must be one which is applied to an article and must be novel in the sense of being new (s 1(2)).

Section 44(1) provides that 'article' means any article of manufacture and includes any part of an article if that part is made and sold separately.

In *Ford Motor Co Ltd's Design Applications* [1995], the House of Lords held that an article should be an independent item intended to be made and sold individually, rather than part of a larger article.

The EC Design Directive contains a radically different definition of article: '. . . any industrial or handicraft item intended to be assembled into a complex product, packaging, get-up, graphic symbols and typographical typefaces, but excluding computer programmes.' A complex article itself is one 'which is composed of multiple components which can be replaced permitting disassembly and re-assembly of the product'. On this basis, *Ford Motor Co Ltd's Design Application* [1995] would become redundant.

The design right is owned by the person who created it (s 2(1)).

The owner of the design right enjoys exclusive rights in relation to articles encompassing the design. An exclusive licensee has no right to sue for infringement of a registered design (*Isaac Oren v Red Box Toy Factory* [1999]).

Infringement is determined by viewing the article through the eyes of the interested consumer.

The right subsists for an initial period of five years, renewable at five yearly intervals to a maximum of 25 years.

UNREGISTERED DESIGN RIGHTS UNDER THE COPYRIGHT, DESIGNS AND PATENTS ACT (CDPA 1988)

An unregistered design right is created under s 213(2) of the CDPA 1988.

Under s 213, 'design' means: '... the design of any aspect of the shape or configuration (whether external or internal) of the whole or part of the article'.

The owner of the unregistered design right is entitled to exclusive rights of reproduction. The owner must establish either copying of the design or a substantial part of it (s 226(2)).

Secondary infringement may arise under s 227(1).

To qualify for protection, a design must:

▨ be recorded in a document after 1 August 1989;

▨ be original;

▨ not be subject to exclusion;

▨ qualify for protection under s 213(5).

Where an article is made to a design in which the design right subsists or has subsisted, the court will act on the presumption that the article was made at a time when the right subsisted, unless the contrary can be proved.

Originality requires that the design must not be commonplace in the area of design in question (s 213(4)) and must originate with the designer and not have been copied. (See *C and H Engineering v Klucznic* [1992].)

The design right subsists in the design for 15 years from when it was recorded in a document, unless articles have been made available for sale, in which case the period is limited to 10 years.

A number of exceptions exist, under s 213, to the entitlement to protection.

The design right will not arise in the following excluded categories under s 213:

(a) principles of construction;

(b) where the article has features that enable it to be connected, placed in or around another article to perform a function ('must fit');

(c) designs that depend on the appearance of another article ('must match');

(d) surface decoration.

Exceptions (b) and (c) are particularly relevant to the manufacturers of spare parts.

Excluded categories under s 213:

■ method or principle of construction;
■ shapes or configurations which are functional ('must fit');
■ dependent on appearance of another item ('must match');
■ surface decoration.

You should now be confident that you would be able to tick all of the boxes on the checklist at the beginning of this chapter. To check your knowledge of Design rights why not visit the companion website and take the Multiple Choice Question test. Check your understanding of the terms and vocabulary used in this chapter with the flashcard glossary.

Remedies

Intellectual property rights were traditionally enforced through the courts. However, under the Woolf Reforms alternative dispute resolution is encouraged, while the World Intellectual Property Organization (WIPO) has an Arbitration and Mediation Centre for international bodies.

A range of orders and remedies are available, the most important of which are:

▓ injunctions, which need to be considered in almost every case; and

▓ damages.

INJUNCTIONS

Injunctions are orders from the courts, prohibiting a party from pursuing a wrongful course of conduct.

Injunctions are equitable and given at the discretion of the court.

WHAT IS A FINAL INJUNCTION?
Final or perpetual injunctions are made at the finale of court proceedings, the relevant evidence pertaining to the case will have been heard in its entirety and the court will have had sufficient time to consider all the relevant issues.

WHAT IS A NEGATIVE INJUNCTION?
Most injunctions are negative in character; the name is apt as negative injunctions are orders which can be complied with by the respondent not undertaking the act which is prohibited.

WHAT IS A POSITIVE INJUNCTION?
Positive injunctions comprise an order that is complied with by the infringing party undertaking the order handed down by the court. A positive injunction can resemble an order for the remedy of specific performance; however, this type of injunction is not commonly seen in the area of interim injunctions.

ARE THERE ANY ALTERNATIVES TO INJUNCTIONS?
A party can, as a potential alternative to the threat of a court-mandated injunction, enter into an undertaking; this was seen in *Beckham v News of the World*

[2005]. In an undertaking the party (consensually) promises to carry out or abstain from a specified act or acts. If this promise is breached, the subsequent enforcement of undertakings run along similar lines to injunctions in the area of patent infringement.

The interim (formerly called interlocutory) injunction is the most frequently used pre-trial order and is the preferred remedy in most cases, as it prevents an infringer from exploiting the intellectual property of another.

As in most civil cases, an intellectual property dispute may not go as far as trial, and a case will often be settled by negotiation or a licensing agreement.

The leading case is *American Cyanamid v Ethicon* [1975], which involved a patent for a dissolving medical stitch.

It was held that, in determining whether to grant an interlocutory injunction or not (that is, the exercise of the court's discretion), the following factors must be addressed:

- Is there a serious issue to be tried?

- Can the claimant show a strong *prima facie* case?

- Would damages be a suitable remedy for the claimant?

- Could the claimant, if unsuccessful, adequately compensate the defendant with damages?

- Does the 'balance of convenience' favour one party or the other? If even, then the status quo will be preserved and the application refused.

Injunctions – relevant factors:

- discretionary;
- serious issue;
- damages not a remedy;
- balance of convenience;
- status quo.

Generally, the courts will act to preserve the status quo and grant the injunction in favour of the claimant.

Damages will not be a suitable remedy where the wrong is:

(a) **irreparable;**

(b) **outside the scope of financial compensation;**

(c) **very difficult to calculate (for example, damage to reputation).**

See diagram on facing page.

In *American Cyanamid*, it was considered less harmful to restrain a new activity than to undermine an established one. In *Cayne v Global Natural Resources plc* [1984], the balance of convenience was taken to mean the balance of the risk of doing injustice.

The penalties for a wilful breach of an injunction are: fine, imprisonment or sequestration of assets (*DGFT v Smith's Concrete* [1991]).

Inability to pay damages due to financial weakness may be a reason to grant an injunction (*Missing Link Software v Magee* [1989]).

In *Series 5 Software v Philip Clarke and Others* [1995], reviewing these principles, the court stated the discretionary nature of injunctive relief. It was emphasised that the court should not try to resolve difficult matters of fact and law at an early stage. If the strength of a party's case can be assessed at the interim stage, it should be taken into account in deciding whether to grant relief.

Injunctions in the form of disclosure orders may be granted against a non-infringer in intellectual property cases – the so-called 'Norwich Pharmacal orders'.

In *Norwich Pharmacal Co v Comrs of Customs and Excise* [1974], a court order was granted against a non-infringer so that names and addresses of those responsible for distributing infringing goods had to be disclosed. A defence of confidentiality will not succeed (see also *Coca-Cola and Others v BT plc* [1999]). Now the Civil Procedure Rules 1998 r 31 may be used to obtain the same outcome.

A claimant may obtain an injunction against an innocent defendant dealing with infringing items (*Microsoft v Plato Technology* [1999]).

Interlocutory injunction

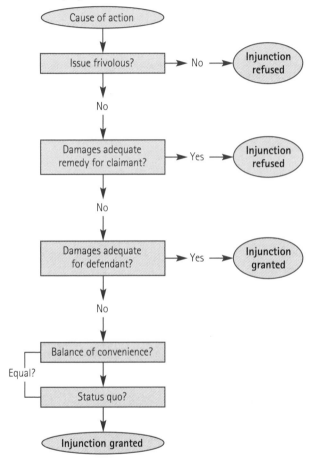

The courts may refuse an injunction where a transaction is an isolated one and there is no likelihood of repetition (*Leahy, Kelly and Leahy v Glover* [1893]).

Further principles that a court may apply in relation to final injunctions are set out in *Shelfer v City of London Electric Lighting Co* [1895]. Relief may be denied if:

- the injury to the claimant's legal rights is small;

- it is one which is capable of being estimated in money;

- it is one which can be adequately compensated by a small money payment; and

- it would be oppressive to the defendant to grant an injunction.

Damages in substitution for an injunction may then be given. The purpose of an injunction may also be considered to be not to stop a continued flow of a wrongful benefit arising from the breach, but to prevent a continuation of the breach of confidence.

PRE-TRIAL ORDERS

A search order (formerly called an Anton Piller order) allows the seizure of infringing goods or documents where there is a danger that a defendant may hide or destroy the evidence.

In *Anton Piller KG v Manufacturing Processes* [1975], Ormrod J held that a claimant must be able to show:

- a strong *prima facie* case;

- the damage, whether actual or potential, must be very serious for the claimant; and

- there must be clear evidence that the defendants have, in their possession, documents or objects and that there is a real possibility they may destroy such materials.

In *Columbia Picture Industries v Robinson* [1986], it was held that the claimant must show a strong case for infringement of his rights and that potential damage is serious. Also, in *Chappell v UK* [1989] a challenge to an Anton Piller order was made in the European Court of Human Rights arguing breach of the privacy guarantee under Art 8. The action failed. However, care must be taken when serving a search order as any abuse will invalidate it (see *Universal Thermosensors v Hibben* [1992]; *Practice Direction* [1994] and the Civil Procedure Act 1997).

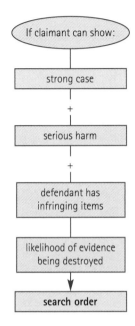

DAMAGES

Damages are often sought by claimants in intellectual property cases, in addition to injunctions.

Damages are generally available for all breaches of intellectual property rights, though they may be limited by statute and case law. The measure of damages is normally tortious, that is, the aim is to put the injured party back in the position he would have enjoyed had the injury never taken place (*General Tire and Rubber Co v Firestone* [1975]). However, a claimant can only claim losses caused by the defendant's wrongful acts that are a reasonably foreseeable result of his actions.

Factors that may be considered in assessing damages are:

▧ whether the claimant would have charged a licence fee for the work; and

▧ whether he would have expected a royalty.

ACCOUNT OF PROFITS

As an alternative to damages, the claimant may claim an account of profits, an equitable remedy whereby the claimant claims the profit that the defendant has made on each infringing item.

An account of profits recovers the unjust enrichment that the defendant has obtained. It is a technical and expensive remedy, involving professional scrutiny of accounts. Difficulties may arise with establishing the date from which the assessment may run (see *Potton v Yorkshire* [1990]).

DELIVERY UP

Where a claimant obtains a final injunction, the courts may include an order for delivery up of the infringing articles.

See ss 99, 230 of the Copyright, Designs and Patents Act (CDPA) 1988; s 61 of the Patents Act (PA) 1977; ss 15–19 of the Trade Marks Act (TMA) 1994.

The order may also encompass the destruction of the goods or the obliteration of an offending mark from goods.

CRIMINAL SANCTIONS

In addition to civil remedies, the law provides criminal sanctions for various infringing acts.

A claimant is entitled to take civil action and commence criminal proceedings simultaneously (*Thames and Hudson Ltd v Design and Artists Copyright Society Ltd* [1995]; *R v Bridgeman and Butt* [1995]).

Criminal sanctions exist as follows:

- copyright: ss 107–10, 198, 207, 297–297A of the CDPA 1988;

- trade marks: s 92 of the TMA 1994;

- patents: ss 110–11 of the PA 1977.

You should now be confident that you would be able to tick all of the boxes on the checklist at the beginning of this chapter. To check your knowledge of Remedies why not visit the companion website and take the Multiple Choice Question test. Check your understanding of the terms and vocabulary used in this chapter with the flashcard glossary.

11

Putting it into practice...

Now that you've mastered the basics, you will want to put it all into practice. The Routledge Questions and Answers series provides an ideal opportunity for you to apply your understanding and knowledge of the law and to hone your essay-writing technique.

We've included one exam-style essay question, which replicates the type of question posed in the Routledge Questions and Answers series to give you some essential exam practice. The Q&A includes an answer plan and a fully worked model answer to help you recognise what examiners might look for in your answer.

QUESTION 1

Critically analyse the traditional justifications for the existence of the systems of intellectual property protection.

Answer plan

This question requires the student to demonstrate an appreciation of the various theories for justifying the granting of monopolistic intellectual property protection rights:

- 'Natural rights'; John Locke's Labour theory (1632–1704);
- Art 27(2) of the Universal Declaration of Human Rights;
- Hegel's Personality theory (1770–1831);
- Economic justification and the Utilitarian theory;
- Consumer protection.

Answer

Legal and political philosophers have often debated the status and legitimacy of intellectual property. They ask, 'Why should we grant intellectual property rights?' The answer to this question is important, because society has a choice as to whether it chooses to grant such rights. It is also important because the decision to grant property rights in intangibles impinges on traders, the press and media and the public.

Intellectual property rights have three key features. First, they are property rights. Secondly, they are property rights in something intangible. Thirdly, they protect innovation and creations and reward innovative and creative activity. All intellectual property rights have one common feature: for any subject matter to be protected by an intellectual property right, the minimum criteria for that form of property must be met.

On the one hand, the grant of private property rights in land and tangible resources is premised on the scarcity or limited availability of such resources and the impossibility of sharing. However, how can we justify the grant of exclusive rights over ideas and information – that are not scarce and can be replicated without any direct detriment to the original possessor of the intangible (who continues to be able to use the information)?

A central characteristic of intellectual property rights is that they are negative monopolistic rights. They exclude others from the use and exploitation of the subject matter of the right. However, all intellectual property rights expire at some point in time, except for confidential information, trade marks and geographical indications, which can be perpetual.

Intangible property rights are fundamentally different from rights attaching to tangible property such as a house, a car or a piece of jewellery. The subject matter of intellectual property rights, creative endeavour and inventions, necessarily has a link with knowledge and ideas. In economic terms, such matter is a public asset not easily owned by one person or group. The ability to exclude others from use or copying arises due to an artificial legal regime which grants an intangible property right to the inventor or creator.

As we will see, philosophers have not always found intellectual property rights to be justified in the form they currently take. Why are intangible property rights created? The existence of intellectual property rights is usually justified by reference to one or more of the following grounds.

(1) Natural rights
One of the most basic justifications for intellectual property is that a person who puts intellectual effort into creating something should have a natural right to own and control what he creates. This is derived from the 'Labour theory' by the seventeenth-century philosopher John Locke. He argued that everyone has a property right in the labour of his own body, and that the appropriation of an

unowned object arises out of the application of human labour to that object. There must remain objects of similar quality in sufficient quantity to supply others. In other words, 'He who sows shall also reap'. Such an entitlement is recognised in Art 27(2) of the Universal Declaration of Human Rights, which states:

> Everyone has the right to the protection of moral and material interests resulting from any scientific, literary or artistic production of which he is the author.

In addition, according to Georg Hegel's Personality theory, 'Creation is an extension of its creator's individuality or person, belonging to that creator as part of his or her selfhood'.

(2) To encourage and reward innovation and creation
Intellectual property rights serve as an incentive for the investment of time and capital in the research and development which are required to produced inventive and creative works. By providing the owner with exclusive property rights, he enjoys the benefit of the stream of revenue generated by exploitation of his intellectual property.

(3) To encourage dissemination of information and ideas
The existence of intellectual property laws encourages the disclosure and dissemination of information and widens the store of knowledge available in the community. This justification is commonly given for patents. The specification of patented inventions are published by patent offices around the world and form a valuable source of advanced technical information.

(4) Economic efficiency
Economic theorists justify the recognition of property rights in creative endeavour on the basis that it leads to more efficient use of resources. Innovation is an essential element in a competitive free market economy. Economists argue that if everyone was freely allowed to use the results of innovative and creative activity, the problem of 'free riders' would arise. Investors would be reluctant to invest in innovation. Competitors would just wait for someone else to create a product, which they would then copy at little upfront cost. Legal protection of intangible property rights creates a climate in which investors are stimulated to invest in research and development, as they will be guaranteed a competitive 'first to market' advantage for a period of time.

(5) Consumer protection
Some intellectual property rights offer protection for consumers by enabling them to make informed choices between goods and services from different sources (for example, trade marks and geographical indications).

(6) Technology transfer
Intellectual property systems facilitate the transfer of technology through foreign direct investment, joint ventures and licensing.

In conclusion, intellectual property law attempts to strike a balance between:

■ the conflicting interests of society as a whole in economic and cultural development;

and

■ the interest of the individual to secure a 'fair' value for its intellectual effort or investment of capital or labour.

This continual tension leads scholars to constantly evaluate the philosophical, economic and ethical justifications of the systems for granting intellectual property rights.

ROUTLEDGE STUDENT STATUTES

PUBLIC LAW AND HUMAN RIGHTS STATUTES 2011–2012

■ Un-annotated – trusted for both course and exam use
■ Up-to-date and compiled by experienced authors
■ Selected based on current research

PHILIP JONES

The best value and best format books on the market.

– Ed Bates, Southampton University, UK

2011–2012 Editions Available Now!

Completely Updated

visit our website for more details

Routledge Student Statutes present all the legislation students need in one easy-to-use volume.

- **Exam Friendly**: un-annotated and conforming to exam regulations
- **Tailored to fit your course**
- **Trustworthy**: Routledge Student Statutes are compiled by subject experts, updated annually and have been developed to meet student needs through extensive market research
- **Easy to use**: a clear text design, comprehensive table of contents, multiple indexes and highlighted amendments to the law make these books the more student-friendly Statutes on the market
- **Competitively Priced**: Routledge Student Statutes offer content and usability rated as good or better than our major competitor, but at a more competitive price
- Supported by a **Companion Website** filled with extra resources

www.routledgelaw.com/statutes

Available from all good bookshops

Subjects covered include:

■ Company Law
978-0-415-68745-4

■ Contract, Tort and Restitution
978-0-415-68744-7

■ Criminal Law
978-0-415-68305-0

■ Employment Law
978-0-415-68645-7

■ European Union Legislation
978-0-415-68688-4

■ Evidence
978-0-415-68729-4

■ Family Law
978-0-415-68461-3

■ International Trade Law
978-0-415-68659-4

■ Property
978-0-415-68369-2

■ Public Law and Human Rights
978-0-415-68743-0

Routledge
Taylor & Francis Group